THIS IS HOW WE DO

How Women Work Through Obstacles to
Get Into Executive and Board Positions

LIZ MAKOMA DITSHEGO

COPYRIGHT

THIS IS HOW WE DO

Copyright © Liz Makoma Ditshego 2015

Print ISBN: 978-0-620-65423-4

eBook ISBN: 978-1-329-21414-9

Layout, eBook conversion and distribution by www.bulabuka.co.za

Contacts:

Postal address: P. O. Box 12743, Vorna Valley, 1686

Email: lizditshego3@gmail.com

Mobile: +27 83 209 0148

CONTENTS

DEDICATION

"What counts in life is not that we have lived. It is what difference we have made to the lives of others that will determine the significance of the life we lead"

— Nelson Mandela (1918-2013), South African anti-apartheid revolutionary, politician, activist, lawyer, philanthropist and first democratically elected President of South Africa.

Julio Iglesius has dedicated a song "to all the girls I've loved before". Beyoncé has dedicated a song to "all the single ladies". And me? I dedicate this book to all the women who aspire to become members of executive suites and boards of corporate organizations South Africa and elsewhere. I hope it will inspire your ambition, ignite your will power and set

you on a path to immense success as future female leaders.

INTRODUCTION

"Women hold up half the sky" — Mao Tse-Tung,

but "Women are the most underutilised resource in the planet" — Hillary Clinton

A huge body of research has been conducted to find out why there are still so few women in the top echelons of management in corporates and governments around the world. Although women are now able to access these positions, progress is very slow. It is clear that there are obstacles that women who want to access executive positions face. But how can women navigate through these barriers to get ahead?

In my research, I sought to get to the bottom of this. I interviewed women in EXCO level positions, or the C-Suite (as others call it), to find out what obstacles they faced in their career paths and how they worked through them to achieve success.

The aim of this book is to empower women, particularly those in middle to senior management, by teaching them how to work through barriers and position themselves for promotion into the C-Suite.

The title of the book – "THIS IS HOW WE DO" – captures the essence of the book beautifully. The book is simply about sharing how other women have worked through the obstacles

that women face in the workplace and have advanced their careers into the C-Suite.

My daughters were thrilled about the title, as they are madly in love with songs by Katie Perry and Rita Ora, both titled "THIS IS HOW WE DO". They thought I am such a cool mum, to name my book after cool songs by cool and young music artists. Little did they know that this was just a pure coincidence, that their mum had no idea who these artists were or that these two songs even existed. Nevertheless, I played along. I am such a cool mum.

OVERVIEW

In an effort to address the shortage of women in top management, South African policy makers have introduced various pieces of legislation and policies, including the BBBEE (Broad-Based Black Economic Empowerment) Act (53/2003) and its amendments, and the Employment Equity Act 47 of 2013. Gender equality is also embedded into the South African constitution and is protected by the Gender Equality Commission. Furthermore, women have been classified as Previously Disadvantaged Individuals (PDIs) – a classification that recognises that those who fall under it have been treated unfairly prior to the dawn of democracy, and therefore must be prioritised for economic redress.

Recently, the Government has passed the Women's Empowerment and Gender Equality (WEGE) Bill (50/2013), which calls for the progressive realisation of at least 50% representation of women in all decision-making structures – including top management – into law. WEGE seeks to dramatically accelerate women advancement. It is yet to be seen if this new piece of legislation will realise its objective.

The 2014 Department of Labour's Commission for Employment Equity (CEE) report shows that 46% of the economically active population are women. This is good news, as it means that we are nearing a 50-50 mark, where as many women as men are employed. However, before we beat the drum and begin celebrating, let us ponder on another statistic, which comes as a big letdown, and that is the fact that, although many women are joining the workforce, they get stuck in middle management. Very few of them make it to top management.

This is evident in the CEE report, which shows that 30% of economically active women are in senior management, but only 20.6% are in top management. In the ten years between 2003 and 2013, the number of women in top management has only grown by 6.6%. Around the world, the situation is not much different. A 2012 McKinsey study titled *Unlocking the Full Potential of Women at Work* found that out of nearly 140 000 women who have already made it to mid-level management at the companies that were surveyed, only about 7 000 have become members of the C-suite.

The fact that most women get stuck in senior management can be explained by two reasons. The first is a leaky pipeline. When I graduated from the Wits Business School with a Postgraduate Diploma in Management (PDM) in 1994, a couple of organizations came onto campus to scout for talent. As many women as men were recruited into entry level positions. I was one of these graduate employees. I was twenty-one when I landed my first job. By the time we were twenty-three to twenty-five years old, myself and a lot of the other people who were employed at the same time (both men and women) had managed to move from graduate employees to junior management and by twenty-five to thirty we had moved into senior management. Promotions into senior management happened simultaneously with marriage and the starting of families. Once they became mothers, most of the women chose to focus on raising them, instead of pushing for career advancement into top management. Men, on the other hand, went on to access top management positions, despite having young children.

The second reason why most women get stuck in senior management is the lack of confidence by women that they will ever make it into top management. Yes. Some women have no ambition to get into top management and are happy to stay in middle management. However, the majority of them do have ambitions of accessing the C-Suite. A McKinsey (2013) report titled *Women Matter*, found that 79% of women do have ambitions to enter into top management positions. The same report shows, however, that only 58% of those in junior management and 69% of those in senior management believe that they will ever get into the C-Suite. Why?

These women have been faced with barriers that make it seem impossible to get ahead. They believe that those who manage to access those positions are either lucky or have a magic wand. Slaughter (2012), in her much-read *Atlantic* magazine piece, *Why Women Still Can't Have it All*, beautifully summed up how these women in middle management, particularly those with children, feel. She said: It's time to stop fooling ourselves, the women who have managed to be both mothers and top professionals are superhuman, rich, or self-employed. Due to this belief, hard-won advances to the executive committee are often followed by departures.

I challenge this view. The women who have managed to reach top management (at least the ones that I have interviewed) are not superhuman. Yes, they may be rich, as they have worked hard on their careers, but they seemed like normal human beings when I interacted with them. And yes, they may have been lucky, but *"the amount of good luck coming your way depends on your willingness to act"* (Barbara Sher). Instead of relying on sheer luck alone, they took action to work through barriers and get where they are today.

But how did they do it? This is where this book comes in. It will show how top-achieving women have worked through obstacles to access C-Suite positions. The book offers advice from successful women who sit on EXCOs and Boards, in South Africa and elsewhere in the world, including the women that I interviewed in my research; as well as from renowned academics and researchers.

As will emerge as one goes from chapter to chapter, there is no single strategy that women who want to access the C-Suite can adopt. Instead, there are a variety of approaches. It is important too, to note that the career paths of women differ from one person to another. Just as everyone's life journey is unique, everybody's career path is different. What worked for Rebecca is not what worked for Elizabeth. However, the pieces of advice in this book are based on what worked for the majority of top women executives.

1. WHY WOMEN MATTER

First things first. Before we continue, let's find out why the issue of having women in top management is receiving so much attention. Have men not been doing a good enough job up there, on their own? Why do we need women at the top?

Over the past few decades, there has been mounting pressure from academics, governments and women's movement groups alike, to increase the number of women in top management. The motivation for this goes beyond the mere need to uplift women and rectify the scourge of gender inequality. There has been a realisation that having women at the top actually has a positive effect on a firm's performance. Globalisation has brought in new challenges for C-Suite executives. The world of business has suddenly become complex and interconnected. Gone are the days when one executive was able to single-handedly resolve a multi- dimensional corporate challenge. Today, the key word to solving complex business issues is *collaboration*.

Collaboration is associated with patience, humility, flexibility and empathy – qualities that are essential for effective leaders. All these qualities are found in women's natural leadership style. Women may be seen as especially attractive candidates to guide organizations because they are perceived as utilizing a leadership style that promotes openness and inclusion, and facilitates change (Furst and Reeves 2008). Therefore, it goes without saying that women are the future leaders who will drive business forward and ensure sustainability.

In addition, Vinkenburg, van Engen et al. (2011) argue that women score higher in transformational leadership – which is essential for managing complexity – than men do. Transformational leaders inspire their followers to achieve more. They set expectations and achieve greater results by challenging their followers to be more innovative. They help bring about major, positive changes by moving group members beyond their self-interest and towards the good of the group, organization or society (DuBrin 2010).

Furthermore, other research has established that all of the aspects of leadership style on which women exceeded men relate positively to leaders' effectiveness, whereas all of the aspects on which men exceeded women have negative or null relations to effectiveness (Eagly and Johannesen- Schmidt 2001).

The case for having women in top management is also made by Barsh and Yee (2012) in a Wall Street Journal article that cites a McKinsey Report titled *Unlocking the Full Potential of Women at Work*, where they state that the prize for making gender diversity in top management a priority is *a talent advantage that's hard to replicate*. The two authors maintain that diversity of thought thrives in such places, fuelling creativity and innovation. Women, men, and their companies benefit as more talent rises to the top. In a nutshell, diverse leadership generates stronger business results.

Helping talented women develop and advance promises significant economic benefit to companies. A McKinsey (2013) report titled *Women Matter* has revealed that companies with more women in top management positions tend to exhibit better organizational and financial performance. The report shows that companies with top quartile representation of women in executive committees (EXCOs) perform significantly better than companies with no women at all. These companies reported increases of 47% in average return on equity and 55% average earnings before interest and tax.

Dezsö and Ross (2012) also found that a given firm generates on average 1% (or over $40 million) more economic value with at least one woman on its top management team than without any women on its top management team and also enjoys superior accounting performance. We believe that these results make a powerful business case for gender diversity and suggest that a CEO who goes the extra mile to help women overcome barriers to their managerial advancement will often be rewarded with improvements in firm performance.

Women are also better than men in creating business sustainability, because they are more sensitive to ethical issues. In their study, Kray and Hasselhuhn (2012) found that men's lower ethical standards in business negotiations are driven in part by their desire to prove their masculinity (if negotiations are a "man's game", then the implication is that men who are not at the top of the pecking order are somehow less manly).

Indeed, if we consider the latest corporate scandals that were rooted in corruption and unethical behaviour, such as the Enron saga, the scoundrels are mostly men. There are, of course, unethical business women as well, such as Martha Stewart of ImClone, but they are few and far between when compared to men.

The importance of achieving better gender balance at all levels of organizations is also being advocated by the 30% Club, which aims to have at least a 30% women representation in board and top management levels of big companies, by the end of 2015. Sir Philip Hampton, Chairman of The Royal Bank of Scotland and a Club member, said: "First, if we don't have more senior women we aren't getting a sufficient contribution from some of our most able people. Second, you're less likely to get the breadth of input to critical discussions and decisions if you only access one gender."

It is heartening to see that more and more organizations are now heeding the call to incorporate diverse backgrounds and experiences and building consciousness in how people approach business problems and leadership. They have begun to realise that when a critical mass of high-performing men and women middle managers strive to grow and contribute at higher levels, the company builds an advantage that's among the hardest for competitors to copy. They have woken up to the fact that:

"Some leaders are born women". Geraldine Ferraro

2. THE 'GLASS-CEILING' IS NO LONGER THE CULPRIT

The 'glass-ceiling' is a label that was first introduced by Carol Hymowitz and Timothy Schellhardt, in a 1986 Wall Street Journal. This was the era when more women managed to enter the work place in entry level positions and slowly progressed to middle management, but were overlooked for executive positions because of their reproductive capacity. It was feared that they would leave work to go on maternity leave. Those who already had young children or disclosed their intentions to have them were penalised.

Although the number of women in top management is still lower than the desired 30%, more women are becoming more and more noticed for their exceptional success in the male-dominated corporate world of global business. A number of successful women have finally been able to climb up the corporate ladder, arriving at high-ranking positions in some of the most renowned corporations of the world. This implies that the "glass-ceiling", once considered the biggest barrier for women to entering the C-Suite, has been broken. As Barreto, Ryan et al. (2009) put it, since the term "glass- ceiling" was first coined, women have made great progress. On the front page of an article in a 2004 Wall Street Journal written by Carol Hymowitz, titled *Through the Glass Ceiling*, there were the faces of fifty women who Hymowitz (2004) said had broken the glass-ceiling. Among them were Carli Fiorina (CEO of Hewlett-Packard since 1999), who said "My appointment proves that we are at a point were everyone has figured out that there is not a glass ceiling". A (McKinsey 2013) report also found that the scarcity of women in top management is not due to a glass-ceiling, but is a result of a leaky pipeline.

In South Africa too, women have long managed to break through barriers and access the C-Suite. Over the last decade, a younger breed of female corporate executives has also found its way into the highest level of management in corporate South Africa. These include some of the women that I interviewed for my thesis and the ones that I surveyed outside my thesis for the purpose of this book, including CEOs, MDs, GMs, CFOs, COOs, Marketing Directors, HR Directors, Chief Risk Officers and Chief Compliance Officers. If you are a woman in middle to senior management, with ambitions to enter the C-Suite, you should be smiling right now, as you should have figured out that there is definitely a chance for you to get into top management.

By now, you should know that:

1. Women do matter in top management, and companies and governments have noticed that.

2. The South African government is serious about the agenda of getting more women there. Pro-women legislation, including the new WEGE policy prove this. In addition, South Africa was placed in the 18th place in the World Economic Forum's report – The Global Gender Gap – which ranks 142 countries on the economic participation of women WEF (2013). This ranking places South Africa ahead of countries such as Canada (19th place) and the US (20th place), a reinforcement that South Africa is determined to close the gender gap.

3. Women currently only make up 21% of top management in South Africa. The ideal composition, according to the WEGE

18

policy, is 50%. This means that you still have a great chance of fulfilling your dream.

4. The time of "glass-ceiling" is over

5. Now, more than ever before, South Africa has many opportunities for women executives.

So, if you really want that title that starts with "Chief... Officer", you can have it. Your time is now. Learn from other women as they say to you in this book: THIS IS HOW WE DO.

3. RAISE YOUR HAND FOR LINE JOBS AND RISKY ASSIGNMENTS

According to Ibarra (2012)'s 70 – 20 – 10 rule, 70% of a manager's learning and development should come from on-the-job learning through stretch assignments (line role responsibilities), 20% from mentoring and 10% from classroom learning.

De Pater, Van Vianen et al. (2010) point out that lack of access to developmentally relevant role experiences can seriously retard female career progress. I too found that access to (and success in) line role responsibilities is crucial for women who want to advance to top management, particularly for those who want to attain C-Suite positions with responsibilities directly linked to the bottom line, such as CEO, CFO and MD. This reinforces the argument by Day and Harrison (2007) that job assignments, particularly those in line roles involving shared work and defined by the number and degree of interdependencies among subordinates, are developmentally essential.

Furthermore, line role positions give the incumbent control over both the revenue and cost functions of a business unit, while giving the person greater opportunitiesnto expand their social capital (Bilhuber Galli and Müller- Stewens 2012). De Pater, Van Vianen et al. (2010) maintain that the experience gained in line roles is a major factor in building valuable capital and overcoming the gender disparity in executive and CEO roles.

Unfortunately for women, exposure to line roles is limited. It has been suggested that one reason so few women have been promoted to top management positions is that during their careers they experience fewer developmental job opportunities than men. Lyness and Thompson (2000) observed that women have more assignments with non- authority relationships. On the other hand, men experience some greater task-related developmental challenges (Ohlott, Ruderman et al. 1994). Additionally, the acquisition of capital can be similarly limited where women are assigned to career paths that are considered more congenial to their stereotypical attributes, such as support functions (Evans and Diekman 2009).

For her World Economic Forum's Corporate Gender Gap Report, Herminia Ibarra (2012), a Professor of Leadership at Insead University, asked the companies that she interviewed the following question: "Among the assignments that you consider to be business critical/important, what percentage, in your opinion, are currently held by women (e.g. key start- ups, turnarounds, and line roles in key business units or markets)?" The most common answers were "0-10%" or "not measured". Ibarra strongly maintains that women's assignments must become the number one priority for committed CEOs who want better results.

Organizations need to focus on their succession planning and know what their "pivotal roles" (those assignments that are deemed essential to an executive's development) are. As this roles are critical in exposing mid-senior managers to the company's primary sources of revenue, strategic markets or key products, it is important that firms actively manage high potentials so that they make their way through a logical progression of these key roles.

It should be noted, however, that while the lack of line role opportunities might be due to an organization's bias towards men, in other cases it is the women themselves who prefer not to pursue and sustain such positions. A McKinsey (2012) study showed that two-thirds of women on Fortune 200 executive committees were in staff roles and that more women than men reported that they would likely move next into support roles. This reinforces the leaky pipeline that was referred to earlier, where women and men are distributed across line and staff roles at similar levels, but women begin a steady shift into staff roles by the time they reach the director level, as line jobs are less flexible than staff jobs for women with families. This means that structurally, women do not have the same opportunities as men to stay in the line. Most women do acknowledge that assuming line role responsibilities would have expedited their chances of accessing the C-Suite and that they would go that route, if they were to start over. Even among the successful women interviewed in the McKinsey 2012 study, there were regrets. More than half felt they held themselves back from accelerated growth. Most said they should have cultivated sponsors earlier because a sponsor would have pushed them to take line opportunities. The women said that they did not raise their hands or even consider stretch roles.

One of life's little pleasures is that we can learn from the regrets of those who have walked the path before us. We are able to learn and grow from others' mistakes. To avoid the regret of not raising your hand to tough but worthy assignments read carefully below.

THIS IS HOW WE DO

Earlier on in your career, preferably before even starting a family, **focus on gaining broad line experience.** More than 80% of the women in my study did exactly that. They employed various strategies to achieve these roles. Consider the following:

Take on international assignments. In my days in the marketing departments of Unilever, Coca-Cola and SC Johnson, a few individuals were given international assignments earlier on in their careers (at Brand Manager and Senior Brand Manager levels). They were seconded to various international offices, including Atlanta, Paris and Switzerland. Today, all these women are in the C-Suite of large multinational FMCG organizations.

Get involved in challenging projects such as designing and implementing turnaround strategies. A large number of my respondents were involved in turnaround processes in their companies. This exposed them to key roles that impact on the profitability of those organizations.

Learn cross-functional responsibilities. Even if you are in a support role, it would help to spend some time in a department that works together with yours, and is a line role function. For example, a Marketing Manager might consider working in a manufacturing plant. This will give them a deep appreciation of production and operations, while broadening their skills. Ursula Burns, the CEO of Xerox advises:

"Along the career path, pursue new skills relentlessly. Change jobs after you've mastered the current one. Be willing to tack sideways on the career track, or even backward, to pick up key expertise or command a business unit".

To sum up this chapter, I quote JACK WELCH at the Women in the Economy conference: ***'To get ahead, raise your hand for line jobs and tough, risky assignments'.***

4. TO SUPPORT YOUR LIFE'S JOURNEY, GET A MENTOR

As per Ibbarra's 70-20-10 principle, mentorship (or sponsorship, as it is commonly referred to in the United States) is the second key ingredient after direct line role responsibilities, for women in accessing the C-Suite.

From when we are young children and at various points in our lives, we all identify and emulate people whom we admire. These are people we want to learn from. We see ourselves living their life at some point. These people are called role models, or mentors in a business environment. That process where our role models take us through a learning process that seeks to mould us into successful individuals is called mentorship. Simply put, mentorship is a close, non-competitive, deeply personal relationship between two people that evolves over time.

In the corporate world, and other spheres of management, mentorship has taken on increased importance, particularly for young managers who are dropped suddenly into new and unfamiliar roles and who face the challenge of high expectations, information overload, and little time to learn to become master of all tasks. In these difficult times of transition, mentors become models for the development of proper problem solving skills, decision-making techniques and interpersonal abilities. More importantly, mentors become valuable in providing personal guidance. The ultimate goal of mentorship is to create an environment that allows new associates to progress as rapidly as possible along the learning curve and mature their management skills. This explains why one of the most popular and oldest pieces of advice for young women who want to build their career into top management is: **find a mentor**.

Mentorship is recommended for women in middle to senior management because over the last decade there has been a general consensus by researchers in both academic and managerial circles that mentorship is a significant career tool, and a prerequisite for career success. Access to a mentor, an older and more experienced career professional who is able to use his or her influence and power in assisting a young and up-and-coming protégé, has been closely associated with career advancement.

While mentorship plays a significant role in both male and female career projection, it seems to be more valuable for females than it is for men. In a recent study by Fitzsimmons, Callan et al. (2014), titled *Gender disparity in the C-Suite: Do male and female CEOs differ in how they reached the top?*, it was found that male CEOs shared a similar view of the importance of role models and described the contribution of these role models to leadership, integrity and stewardship in ways similar to the female CEOs. However, only half of the male CEOs credited mentors with having made a key difference in their career progression. Only a few mentioned mentors as having been instrumental in providing advice that promoted their confidence to apply for key roles that led to their appointments as CEOs.

There are also women executives who do not credit mentorship and mentors to their career success. While the $70-20-10$ rule places a hefty 20% weighting on mentoring (indicating that mentoring is indeed a crucial component of leadership development), some of my respondents said that mentors were not key in their progression to the C-Suite. Contrary to the popular belief that mentors help to open the door to growth opportunities, counsel them through valleys and peaks and advocate for their advancement, these women did not experience these benefits. They thought of mentoring as a "feel good" exercise or a "nice-to-have" programme.

But why would mentorship be an ineffective intervention for some women's career development? The answer lies in the current, traditional form of mentorship.

Firstly, the traditional mentorship relationship is top- down. The mentor is usually a senior, more experienced (usually male) executive and the mentee is a young and upcoming manager. In such a case, the mentee would go to the mentor for advice if they encounter a challenge and the mentor would offer it. The relationship is a give-and–take relationship, with only the mentee benefiting from it. The mentor sees the mentee only as someone that he or she is helping, not as someone with the potential to contribute to challenging assignments. This may affect the mentor's level of commitment.

Ideally, mentors should see themselves as custodians of leadership and talent development. They should serve their subordinates and view the relationship from a servant leadership perspective. The number one priority for a servant leader is to empower his or her followers. As a mentor, the servant mentor removes him – or herself from the relationship and focuses on the mentee. He or she allows the mentee to take centre stage, and does not have a "what's in it for me" attitude.

In South Africa, according to Cook M et al (1994), servant leadership is not a characteristic of most managers. The authors suggest that in order to change the mind-set that mentorship is a one-way relationship that only benefits mentees, we need to start by changing the vocabulary. Mentorship should be referred to as "a learning partnership". A learning partnership, they argue, entails a quest for learning from which both partners benefit, rather than an unidirectional transfer of knowledge from the mentor to the mentee. *"Giving connects two people, the giver and the receiver, and this connection gives birth to a new sense of belonging."* (Deepak Chopra)

There are companies that have already embraced the concept of learning partnerships, although they refer to it as reverse mentoring or reciprocal mentoring. For example, IBM currently pairs top leaders (often male) with female managers who have been identified as future leaders. The mentor and mentee meet regularly, each learning from the other (Stuckey 2014). The focus is on "learning from each other". Because they interact with them from a win-win angle, the male mentors are willing to expose female leaders to the most strategic work at the company, thus creating visibility for them as up-and-coming top executives.

Secondly, current mentorship arrangements are just informal arrangements between a mentor and mentee. No mentorship contract is entered into. The company might be aware of such arrangements, but may have no systems and processes in place to support and encourage such relationships. This means that there is no commitment from the mentor or the HR department to support the relationship. Because he gets nothing out of the relationship and is not obligated to continue to be in it, he may choose to rather prioritise his work and neglect the mentee, leaving the relationship to fizzle out.

A lot of companies have realised this challenge and have begun to formalise mentorship relationships. For example, Deloitte matches senior leaders (mostly male) to rising female talent for one to two years. The objectives are to build confidence, create visibility of talent internally and provide

Access to stretch assignments. What makes Deloitte's program successful is that the company measures the results of the coaching efforts and holds each coach accountable for the success of his assigned leader in developing new capabilities and expansions of networks. The results are then directly tied to the coach's performance review and compensation (Stuckey 2014).

Lastly, the traditional arrangement involves a mentee identifying a particular individual from their work and approaching them with a mentorship request. The mentee then relies solely on that one person for advice and guidance. This means that the mentee is only exposed to one set of solutions to her career challenges and, because this is an informal arrangement where, unlike in the Delloite case, mentors are not held accountable and measured on how they manage their mentorship relationship, the advice given might not be the best and might not contribute to the development of the mentee.

The mentor might even feel jealous, competitive and threatened by the mentee, especially in cases where the mentee is one level below the mentor. In such cases, the mentee might feel disillusioned and powerless, resulting in the relationship being damaged. A spoiled mentorship relationship will affect how the two individuals work together in a team. If they are not mature enough to deal with it, the entire team might suffer the effects of such a failed relationship.

Sheryl Sandberg's advice is: **"Don't Ask Anyone to be Your Mentor"**. Instead, she advocates asking people, both senior and junior to you, for specific advice to solve a problem. This will engender much more productive relationships than a simplistic, general plea for mentoring.

THIS IS HOW WE DO...

For advice on how to handle a certain project or for feedback on how you chaired an important meeting, I would agree with Sandberg's sentiments. You should not rely on a single mentor. Rather get more than one viewpoint, so that you are in a position to assess for yourself what the best way forward should be.

However, for long-term projects such as career mapping, it is important to get one person to be your mentor. Most importantly, this person should not be from your workplace. In my study, I found that a mentorship relationship that proved most effective and productive was that in which the mentor was from outside the workplace of the mentee. Young managers should consider looking for mentoring networks outside their organizations. By joining professional women's groups that are not directly connected to your workplace, you will learn more about the best practices of others. You will also feel more comfortable talking about challenges and less worried about being judged or seen as a threat.

Companies such as *The Leadership Brewery,* offer a mentoring program whereby mentees are paired up with suitable mentors outside their workplace. The company utilizes a profiling questionnaire to first determine the right style and fit between the mentee and mentor. The mentors are successful women who sit on EXCOs and Boards. They are always ready, able and willing to mentor young, upcoming women as they live by Marrianne Williamson's quote: *"Nothing liberates your greatness like the desire to help, the desire to serve".* This form of mentoring is easier, as it is done among women at different levels and across industries, rather than the one-sided perspective a mentee may get within one company.

Mentors could also be peers outside your work. Consider this example from Bennis, Cherniss et al (2003). A young, Asian associate at a large financial services firm is given feedback in the annual appraisal process that she is perceived as not being assertive enough in her dealings with clients. At a dinner meeting with female peers, she listens to other women speak about their approaches with clients, and she clarifies how her style differs. In reflecting on the feedback and what she heard from her female peers, she becomes aware of how her cultural background influences her professional style. She realizes that what is expected and rewarded at the firm is in conflict with her style. She decides that she would like to try to modify her style and enlists the support of several female peers. She also lets her manager know about this new development.

For me, the biggest lesson about effective mentorship relationships is that as a mentee, as much as you are receiver, you need to show the mentor that you appreciate them giving up their time to mentor you. You should provide them with positive feedback (only if positive feedback is due) and assure them that you see value in what they are offering you. Be careful, though, not to suck up. Just be genuine and make you mentor feel valued.

As I conclude this chapter, I leave you with Maya Angelou's words: "I've learned that people will forget what you said, people will forget what you did, but people will never forget how you made them feel."

5. BE CONFIDENT AND CULTIVATE RISK- TAKING

"I am always doing that which I cannot do, in order that I may learn how to do it." — Pablo Picasso

In her 2013 book titled *Lean In: Women, Work and the Will to Lead*, Facebook COO Sheryl Sandberg says that women keep themselves from advancing because they don't have the self-confidence and drive that men do. "We lower our own expectations of what we can achieve." (Sandberg 2013).

To drive this point home, Sandberg writes about a 2002 survey of medical students in a surgery rotation that showed that women gave themselves lower scores than the men even though faculty evaluations gave the women higher ratings. A 2012 study of thousands of political candidates revealed that the men were 60% more likely to say they were "very qualified" to run for office. A 2004 assessment of Harvard law students found that in skills related to practising law, women gave themselves lower scores than men. Those are just a few of many examples

The confidence-gap, in *Women Matter*, (the Mckinsey report cited earlier) holds that women do have ambition to enter into top management positions, but they do not have the confidence to take up challenging roles and opportunities, as they believe that they will fail. Instead, they pass on these wonderful opportunities and settle for roles that they believe they are comfortable with and will succeed in. A frequently quoted statistic from the confidence-gap is that men apply for jobs when they know they only meet 60% of the requirements, while women apply only when they meet 100%. If a job advert states "an MBA or equivalent is required or desired", a man who is in his first week of a three- year part-time MBA degree will apply. A woman in that same class, will only apply after graduation day in three years' time. And often, the man (because he displays confidence and risk-taking qualities) will be hired.

In addition, The Black Management Forum (BMF) published research a year ago that revealed that female managers are more competent than males, but the majority of women believe that their male counterparts are more effective. They feel less confident and, as a result, they do not take risky appointments.

This is an obstacle because as leadership, as noted by Northouse (2012), involves the ability to influence others and self-confidence allows the leader to feel assured that his or her attempts to influence others are appropriate and right. The positive impact of self-confidence on performance has been shown in a variety of studies. Among supervisors, managers and executives, a high degree of self-confidence distinguishes the best from the average performers.

Bennis, Cherniss et al. (2003) observed in their study that among 112 entry-level accountants, those with the highest sense of self-efficacy, a form of self-confidence, were rated by their supervisors ten months later as having superior job performance. The level of self-confidence was, in fact, a stronger predictor of performance than the level of skill or previous training. In a sixty-year study of more than one thousand high-IQ men and women tracked from early childhood to retirement, those who possessed self- confidence during their early years were most successful in their careers

Thelackofconfidencebywomenisexplainedbyrenowned French sociologist, Pierre Bourdieu (1990), who argues that early life experiences are responsible for the production of social capital that is required in

34

the top echelons of management and leadership roles. The lessons in life begin early, with the influence of family, peers, education, sports and other events of childhood shaping the manager-to-be. The difference in the treatment of boys and girls, particularly in relation to taking risks in childhood play, promotes less self-confidence and self-esteem for women in work contexts. Guay, Marsh et al. (2003) add that gendered personality traits established in childhood may produce disadvantages for women in judgement of their ability to meet promotion.

Fitzsimmons, Callan et al. (2014), found that whilst most men in senior management had the opportunity to understand and develop their leadership through trial and error prior to entering the work environment, many women were developing these experiences on the job. They argue that because leadership mistakes and failures kill confidence, women are therefore not confident enough to take on executive management roles. Women, they maintain, tend to be more risk-averse. Consider one of the greatest male leaders of our times, Steve Jobs. He romanticised risk. Jobs took the biggest risks innovating things that others never thought of. His followers admired him for his courage. "Risk taking adds to the person's ability to influence and lead because others admire such courage." (DuBrin 2010).

I agree that personal motivation and ambition are driven by our internal will, but are also strongly influenced by our earlier life experiences, including the parenting we receive, the friends we make as we grow, the educational opportunities   we get, the networks we form, as well as perceptions, myths and stereotypes that we get exposed to. However, I disagree that being exposed to gender-stereotypes in earlier life determines whether women will have successful careers and ultimately reach top management. The women that I interviewed had various childhood experiences. Some were raised very differently from the boys and other were raised similarly.

When answering my question about whether she was raised similarly or differently from the boys in their households one respondent (a COO of a large corporate bank) said: *"Yes. I grew up differently from boys. Where I grew up was very Afrikaans. Girls needed to follow a career where they could raise kids, such as teaching. Boys were raised to be breadwinners. Parents even took more insurance policies for the boys. The games we played were very different".* Another respondent (a GM at a multinational retail bank) said: *" I am a from a family of three girls. We played no soccer or cricket. That was for boys. Girls did ballet. With career choices, we were expected to move into junior PA roles. For instance, mom got my sister and I to do a secretarial course."*

On the other hand, a respondent who is the MD of a listed insurancehousesaid:"Idon'tthinkIwasraiseddifferentlyfrom boys. I got the same opportunities climbing trees, playing with marbles and dolls. At school, even the choirs were not gender specific." A GM at another bank had the same experience. She said: "At home we were girls only. But I was my father's son. I spent more time with my dad. I would cut grass with him. He told us not to do courses like Public Administration, as we'd have to rely on government for jobs. I went to a girls' school. They were adamant we could be anything we want. I didn't have any ideas that I was a girl".

Outside of my research, there are other women executives who were raised to not feel or think like girls or boys, but to believe that they are their own individuals and that they can achieve anything that they set their minds on. They were taught to question things and look for answers, instead of accepting the norm.

At a 2008 presentation to Wits MBA graduates, Wendy Luhabe, (founder and Chairman at Women Private Equity Fund, South African Entrepreneur, pioneer of economic empowerment initiatives for African women in business) said: *"My parents raised me to challenge and ask questions, not to conform. It is the greatest gift they gave me':*

It may be arguedthatthewomenwhowereraisedsimilarly to boys had a better chance of succeeding to top management than those who were raised differently. However, regardless of these very different childhood experiences, all these female executives have managed to make their way to the C-Suite. Their entry into these positions was not determined by whether they were exposed to gender stereotyping as children or not.

Their experiences as young girls may have shaped them. But it was their ability to rely on themselves that determined their success. Oprah Winfrey once said: "It doesn't matter who you are, or where you came from. The ability to triumph begins with you. Always." Angela Bray, CEO of WellPoint Inc. added to this sentiment: **"The most important factor in determining whether you will succeed isn't your gender, it's you."**

One of the key findings from my research is that it is wise for aspiring leaders to lean in. The women who were exposed to harsh gender stereotyping compensated for those experiences by cultivating risk-taking. They had self- confidence. They were prepared to take risky positions that others did not want. They saw opportunities, where other saw problems. Some of these "ugly" assignments include mergers and acquisitions, as well as re-structuring and turn- around projects.

THIS IS HOW WE DO...

Be prepared to step up to risky assignments that others do not want.

When she was appointed as CEO of Spoornet, Dolly Mokgatle (now Chairperson of Total SA), knew that the state-owned entity was unfunded by government, and that whatever it did had to be funded by its own resources. However, she was willing to take the risk. She leaned in. She said:

"As the head of Spoornet, I walked into an entity with which very few people wanted to be associated at the time. For me, it was a blank canvas

37

because there we no frameworks for success. I loved the idea of turning something ugly into something of which to be proud and behold".

When I asked if their jobs were high-risk jobs or not, one of my respondents (a GM of a retail division of a Health insurance company) said:

"It is high risk. Firstly, my role is new to the organization, but the level of resources and support is inadequate. The impetus to succeed is more on me. I am the one taking the risk". To sum up the important advice in this chapter, I cite the words of Angela Bray, CEO of WellPoint Inc.: **"Be open to opportunity and take risks. In fact, take the worst, the messiest, the most challenging assignment you can find,**

and then take control.

6. EMBRACE SELF-PROMOTION: IT'S OK TO BLOW YOUR OWN HORN

"To get ahead, women need to focus laser-like on performance". These were the words of Jack Welch, former CEO of GE, Speaking at The Wall Street Journal's Women in the Economy Conference, in 2012.

Of course, it goes without saying that performance, which is underpinned by accountability and a very strong work ethic, is expected of managers (not only women, but men too) who want to get ahead. One has to be willing to do whatever it takes to get the job done. There is simply no substitute for hard work when it comes to achieving success. *"One has to set high standards. I can never be happy with mediocre performance."* Patrice Motsepe, South African mining magnate, founder and executive chairman of African Rainbow Minerals, South Africa's richest man in the Sunday

Times annual Rich List 2012.

When Mr. Motsepe said this, he was not speaking about men or women who are employed in his multibillion Rand businesses. He was referring to all the people, particularly those in management, irrespective of their gender. I do not disagree with Jack Welch that performance is the golden key to top management. However, at middle to top management, both men and women are deemed to be great at their jobs already and are equally expected to perform; otherwise they would not be in those positions in the first place. Performance and high standards are equally expected of them.

In fact, a McKinsey 2011 study found that CEOs and senior executives who work with women achievers in top management noted that these women were no different from successful men. Like their male counterparts, these women had a robust work ethic. They were consistently willing to go above and beyond what is asked of them to get the job done. Furthermore, they were results-oriented. They had a relentless focus on performance and improving the bottom line.

Therefore, I disagree with Mr. Welch's view that a single androgynous metric, namely performance, is the only crucial element to career advancement, particularly when it comes to women. The notion that women just need to do a good job and work hard to achieve success to top management is a myth. Here is why I disagree:

Firstly, a McKinsey (2011) report titled *Changing Companies' minds about Women* found that, while men are promoted based on potential, women get a leg up based on past accomplishments. However, even when their past accomplishments are glowing, with the most admirable track record of performance, it is not always easy for women star performers to be noticed. This is because women do not often feel comfortable about blowing their own trumpet about their achievements, or to self-promote.

Self-promotion is another major leadership challenge for women. Although it conveys status and competence, it is not considered to be communal. So, while men can self-promote, modesty is expected even of highly accomplished women. Fitzsimmons, Callan et al. (2014) found that while women expressed having difficulty with the need to self-promote, men use every opportunity to ensure that top management and decision-makers take note of their achievement, thus promoting their visibility to decision-makers

You may have heard a regional sales executive in your office saying loudly and confidently to his counterpart who is responsible for another region, "I have scooped the award for top performing region for the 8th year in a row. I am the man!" This utterance would be met with laughter from everyone in the room. However, if a woman advertising creative director says, "I did it again. I have produced ads that have been winning The Loeries for ten years in succession," she would be given frowns and looked upon as a self-focused, arrogant individual.

In rare cases where you do find women who are comfortable promoting their success, they become less liked. Patriarchy is partly responsible for women's fear of self-promotion. It has taught them to be cautious about appearing to know too much when they are around men, so that men do not see them as a threat. Once male colleagues perceive you as a threat, you risk being disliked, alienated and outcast. But, most of all, you risk facing harsh treatment form them. "Men who feel threatened by women in top positions will do or say things that unsettle us." (Dolly Mokgatle). Let's be honest: the support of male peers is a great confident booster for every woman in a corporate environment.

To make a case in point about women facing the challenge of being disliked, Sandberg (2013) cites one of the most compelling stories, which she calls the Howard/Heidi study. In this story, two professors wrote up a case study about a real-life entrepreneur named Heidi Roizen, describing how she became a successful venture capitalist by relying on her outgoing personality and huge personal and professional network.

The professors had a group of students read Roizen's story with her real name attached and another group read the story with the name changed to "Howard". Then the students rated Howard and Heidi on their accomplishments and on how appealing they seemed as colleagues. While the students rated them equally in terms of success,

41

they thought Howard was likeable while Heidi seemed selfish and not "the type of person you would want to hire or work for". Sandberg's conclusion: when a man is successful, he is well liked. When a woman does well, people like her less. Sandberg herself used to be typical example of how women shy away from their achievements, for fear of being less liked. When she was ranked Number 5 on the list, ahead of First Lady Michelle Obama and Indian politician Sonia Gandhi, in the August 2011 Forbes list of the World's 100 most powerful women, her reaction was: "far from feeling powerful, I felt embarrassed and exposed". She went on to say that she told colleagues that she thought the list was "ridiculous", until her long-time executive assistant, Camille Hart, pulled Sandberg aside and suggested Sandberg was handling the publicity poorly. Forbes editor, Caroline Howard, who covered this story on Forbes.com, said she was most charmed by this anecdote that Sandberg shared (Howard 2011).

Sandberg writes about the conundrum this presents for women. Most of us want to be liked. But if our success means that others don't like us, how motivated are we to do well? Sandberg admits that she has undermined her own accomplishments for fear that others would be turned off. She advises women to overcome the Howard/Heidi stereotype and advocate on their own behalf. She tells a concise story to illustrate her point: At her first performance review with Zuckerberg, six months into her job at Facebook, he told her that her desire to be liked by everyone was holding her back. If you please everyone, he said, you won't change anything. "Mark was right. Everyone needs to get more comfortable with female leaders, including female leaders themselves," she writes.

The inability of some women to self-promote also leads others taking advantage of the situation and claiming the women's successes as their own. For example, a woman might come up with a ground-breaking, innovative concept that dramatically increases revenue for her firm. The concept would be so great that it wins a series of industry awards. Due to the fear or being disliked, the woman might not want to make it public knowledge that it was her concept. A man, on the other hand, often her boss, would not hesitate to jump onto the stage, accept the trophy and say "Thank you for the trophy. As the CEO of this firm, I am very proud of this achievement. It has taken me a lot of blood, sweat and tears to get here. But I finally did it".

THIS IS HOW WE DO

Embrace self-promotion. In addition to performing to the best of their ability, women need to self-promote. Although self-promotion may feel unnatural, women should embrace it and stop worrying that they are drawing too much attention. They should always bear in mind that "Well-behaved women seldom make history." (Laurel Thatcher Ulrich)

Do not entertain the fear of not being liked. Rather focus on being true to yourself and achieving your ambitions for career success. Marianne Williamson put this wisely when she said:

"Our deepest fear is not that we are inadequate. Our deepest fear is that we are powerful beyond measure. It is our light, not our darkness, that most frightens us. We ask ourselves, who am I to be brilliant, gorgeous, talented and fabulous?

"Actually, who are you not to be? You are a child of God. Your playing small doesn't serve the world. There's nothing enlightening about shrinking so that other people won't feel insecure around you. We were born to make and manifest the glory of God that is within us. It's not just in some of us; it's in everyone. And as we let our own light shine, we unconsciously give other people permission to do the same. As we are liberated from our own fear, our presence automatically liberates others."

There are ways to feel more comfortable doing this, including:

Firstly, evaluate your work to pinpoint what differentiates you from other co-workers. In marketing, we differentiate a product or service from its competitors by communicating its USP (Unique Selling Point), the key feature or benefit that makes it stand out from the pack. Once the target market sees value in the uniqueness of the product, they buy it.

The same should apply to young managers. They need to build their own personal brand. Yes. Individuals are brands. Simply put, your personal brand is what people say about you when you are not in the room. Building your own brand starts with establishing what you stand for and what you want to be known for. Once you know what your USP is, you would then need to create an opportunity to use it to stand out from the crowd. You would then need to create you opportunity to show this talent by volunteering to present to top executives.

Let's say you are a good communicator with a great ability to present to all levels of management, but you are not the only person in your team with that gift. There may be some nerd that is able to memorise their slides word for word and engage with their audience without even looking at their presentation.

In such a case, you would need to be clever about how you position yourself as a unique presenter. You may do this by learning the art of storytelling. Telling a story to make your point is a great way to get people to really engage with you and remember your message. To create an even better opportunity to stand out, you could embrace the old adage, "a picture paints a thousand words", and become a visual communicator. People respond well to images, so consider replacing some words in your presentation with graphs and video clips.

Secondly, focus on helping your boss succeed. Find out what projects your manager is working on and offer to lend a hand. Propose solutions for any challenges they may be faced with. In a nutshell, just be helpful and resourceful. The smallest gesture can make a big difference. You could also volunteer to represent your manager in senior meetings that she cannot attend. Familiarise yourself with the items on the agenda. Prepare adequately for the meeting and contribute accordingly to the discussions, but be self-aware of areas in which you are weak.

Thirdly, seize leadership opportunities, no matter how small. Make sure your "let me take that on" attitude extends beyond your relationship with your boss. Raise your hand for new initiatives, especially ones that might be visible to those outside your unit. This will give others a taste of what you'll be like in a more senior role.

Fourthly, don't be a "Miss Know it All". Often, younger and newly qualified managers might feel that they know more than their older colleagues who qualified in the days when dinosaurs lived. For example, an LLB graduate might undermine the experience and qualification of a colleague with a Biuris and expect that only their opinions should be heard. It is unwise to exert authority when you do not have it. Rather focus on what your team wants to accomplish instead of putting yourself first.

Lastly, build relationships. There's an old adage, "It's not who you know, it's who knows you". When you're evaluated for a promotion, it's unlikely your boss will sit in a room alone and contemplate your potential. She'll rely on others to assess your ability, which means you need supporters across the organization — people who are aware of the work you're doing.

Ladies, I cannot stress this enough. **Do not wait to get noticed**. If you do not shout out your achievements and success, no one will. Be careful though, to not engage in unhealthy competitive behaviour. Your efforts to stand out should be about creating a "wow" factor for yourself, and not to step on toes.

I conclude this chapter with Bonnie Marcus' definition of self-promotion, just in case you are still confused and think that I am encouraging you to be an arrogant, self-centred, and pompous individual: *"Self-promotion is a leadership and political skill that is critical to master in order to navigate the realities of the workplace and position you for success."*

— *Bonnie Marcus, The Politics of Promotion: How High- Achieving*

7. FIND A WAY TO NETWORK AND BREAK INTO THE OLD BOYS' CLUB

"More business decisions occur over lunch and dinner than at any other time, yet no MBA courses are given on the subject." – Peter Drucker

Networking, the ability to socialise, establish and maintain relationships in and outside one's professional industry, has been identified by many leadership experts as being an important base for accessing top management positions. Fast-tracked managers spend relatively more time and effort socializing and interacting with outsiders than do their less successful counterparts. Fitzsimmons, Callan et al (2014) found that the great majority of CEO appointments are linked to past associations the candidates has maintained with colleagues and industry professional bodies.

Giscombe (2007) advises that women and men need to ensure that they have appropriate time available to invest in establishing and maintaining meaningful networks. Fitzsimmons, Callan et al. (2014) add that access to networks that are often external to the organization is also essential to test and refine the leadership skills gained through these experiences and to communicate a readiness for higher order experiences.

Men have the "Old Boys' Club", where they tend to network among themselves. Women, on the other hand, do not have such clubs. The Old Boys' Club is exclusive to men, often men in top executive positions. Typically, membership of these clubs is made up of boys who went to the same exclusive, private school or university. Members socialise together, usually by playing golf, having braais (barbecues) and sharing a glass of beer or whiskey. Through these clubs, they share ideas, advise one another and share career-advancement opportunities. Hiring decisions into top management roles are often made through these clubs.

Bourdieu (1990)'s proposition is that every field is dominated by a powerful group of rule makers and enforcers who only grant access to senior levels in that field to those who possess both the personal capital deemed valuable by them and whose lived experiences or "habitus" mirror their own (Fitzsimmons, Callan et al. 2014). What Bourdieu implies is that hiring executives make their decisions on a "similar to me" basis. Reskin and McBrier (2000) argue that, given men's dominance on boards of directors, the tendency is for boards to select males similar to themselves, thereby biasing against the selection of women. A similar-to-me bias is common in hiring decisions.

Holgersson (2001) describes the selection of C-suite executives in terms of co-option, whereby certain informal criteria must be present for the candidate to be accepted into the group. Co-optionprocessesaremorelikelytodisadvantage female candidates because their social experiences are more likely to differ from those of a senior male board member than will the experience of a male candidate.

Eagly and Carli (2007) note that even when women do make time and attempt to network, they are still faced with barriers because the networks tend to be dominated by men who tend to base their networking on masculine activities. The authors cite an example where a female executive at Wal- Mart was once told that she probably would not advance, as she did not hunt or fish. It is simply harder for women to get into the right networks of powerful executives and to cultivate sponsor relationships.

For the majority of my respondents, networking and attending work functions is extremely crucial for their jobs. They attend a lot of these functions, as it is through these functions that they can establish relationships that drive sales and impact on their companies' bottom lines.

Respondent One said: "I attend a lot of work activities. Once a week. Last week I attended two. I go there to look for opportunities to sell. It is absolutely critical for my role. It needs to happen. If you don't attend, you need to find other ways to network to grow the business."

However, for some of the respondents, networking is not all that crucial. They seldom (or never) attended work/ industry-related functions, as they did not see any value in doing so. One respondent said, "Networking is only important if you want to move jobs." Another one said: "Networks make no impact in my career. I've past that stage. My career advancement is in my hands, through studying, learning, sharing etc. Not through networking."

On the question of belonging to professional networks, one respondent said: "I have not found industry bodies to be effective or instrumental in my personal growth and development" (Managing Director of a large, JSE-listed financial services firm). Another respondent said: "I don't belong to formal networks. I believe in personal relationship. I do participate in certain structures where I'm invited as a subject matter expert etc., but I am not a member of a formal body. There are private initiatives that give professionals a chance to network without formalising their association. That way it's more comfortable and it's a space where people share ideas and create opportunities" (Marketing Director at a large JSE-listed media company).

However, for other women, such as the CEO of shipping company, belonging to professional industry bodies and attending networking events is extremely important in her industry. She said: "I belong to the South African Association of Ship Owners and Agents (SAASOA). I attend all networking events organized by the association to meet and connect with peers in the same industry. The association creates a platform of exchange which translates into mirroring yourself, competence wise and making you be ahead of the game."

So, it would seem that the importance and relevance of networking is only crucial in specific sectors such as the shipping industry and the financial services sector, which are still male-dominated. Another interesting finding is that all the respondents who find networking to be critical to their roles are directly responsible for the bottom line. The respondents who do not find networking to be crucial for their jobs occupy support roles.

It can, therefore, be concluded that networking and belonging to networks is only critical to accessing the C-Suite in roles that are directly responsible for generating revenue for the organizations concerned. Women in direct line responsibilities need to network and socialise, as a proactive measure to advance their careers into the C-Suite.

It should be borne in mind, however, that whether you place any value on networking or not, as a woman in a male- dominated industry, your communication style might be one of the things that are blocking your way to the Old Boys Club. It is not uncommon for women in a meeting full of men to want to speak less or to seek the men's approval. They do this as they are afraid that men will not listen to or support them. This deprives women of the opportunity to put their message across effectively.

Humphrey (2014) cites a recent study by a Yale psychologist, Victoria L. Brescoll, which found that male executives received 10% higher ratings of competence from their peers when they spoke more, while female executives who spoke up received 14% lower ratings. Because of the fear of not being listened to or dismissed by men, women tend to seek consensus and approval when they speak. They have a tendency to dismiss their idea if it gets little approval from men, or even apologise for it. Lois Wyse, summed this up nicely when she said: "Men are taught to apologize for their weaknesses, women for their strengths."

THIS IS HOW WE DO...

It is about time that women form their own networking club the Ladies' club. There is nothing stopping women from doing what men are doing, in order to advance their careers. In countries such as Australia and the UK, women have come together and established networking clubs and forums that are exclusive to women. Through these clubs, they share best practice for career success, advise one another and move mountains for fellow members. *The Leadership Brewery* offer such a network, where like-minded female executives work together to advance themselves and other emerging female leaders. Members enjoy exciting networking activities such as learning how to play golf together, playing in golf tournament against men and other women, attending spa retreats, etc.

It should be noted, however, that a women-only network should not be established to compete with the Old Boy's Club. In fact, the two should exist side-by-side and should collaborate. I have found that while it may not be easy for men to grant access to women into their boys' clubs, they are willing to accommodate them if there are common interests between the two clubs. For example, they are willing to play golf with women, if women have an interest in the sport. This is why *The leadership Brewery* has established the ladies golf network, where female members enjoy golf tournaments from time to time with members of the Old Boy's Club. Fun is had by all at these events and so, through golf, women are able to break into the Old Boys' Club.

Attending networking events is also essential for building social capital and powerful networks. Effective networking involves being courageous and getting rid of your nerves. Most women attend a networking event only to sit at the same table as their colleagues or friends and leave immediately after the last speaker ends their speech. While their stomachs and their need to form networks might say yes to the idea of staying on for nibbles and drinks, their nerves say no.

Challenge yourself at the next networking event. Approach a boys' network (group of men) and introduce yourself. The aim is not to talk to all the groups of men in the room. One good-quality conversations with one group is sufficient. Do not feel tempted to talk a lot. Remember that *"the mark of a good conversationalist is not that you can talk a lot. The mark is that you can get others to talk a lot. Thus, good schmoozers are good listeners, not good talkers."* (Guy Kawasaki). Learn to talk to people on public transport. You never know who is sitting next to you in the Gautrain. Find a relevant icebreaker to initiate a conversation. Be careful not to be overbearing. Offer your business card, if you believe the person is the ideal candidate for your network of professionals.

Remember to follow up with all the people you have met up with and interacted with (only if it is worth doing so), if you are serious about having them in your network. You need to put an effort into this exercise and realise that it will not happen overnight. Alan Colins, author of *Unwritten HR Rules*, wrote: *"Pulling a good network together takes effort, sincerity and time."*

Lastly, do not forget to get into social networking. You do not have to be on every social media platform. Facebook is good for telling people what you are eating, so rather choose professional platforms, such as LinkedIn. *"Instead of telling the world what you're eating for breakfast, you can use social networking to do something that's meaningful."* (Edward Norton)

If you do not have to network outside your company, consider networking within your company, particularly if you next career move is an internal promotion. In his article titled *How to become a CEO*, Stadler (2015) holds that the board members of Fortune 100 firms preferred to select internal candidates for CEO positions in 79% of the cases. Similarly, only 11% of the 222 CEOs in the long-living organizations that he studied were outsiders. In the most successful long- living firms, the number was even lower: 3%.

You could break the Old Boys' Club at your office by starting to socialise with the boys. It may feel like you're crashing a party, but make your best effort to socialize with your male co-workers in formal and informal situations. Whether it's tagging along for lunch or drinks after work, important information is exchanged informally; being there to hear it may benefit your career. Generally, when men see that you are making an effort to be part of their club, they will embrace you and welcome you. Their tendency to leave women out of their networks is largely based on an assumption that women would not be interested in male- related activities, such as fishing or golfing, but if they see that their assumption is wrong, they become receptive.

One other way to break into Old Boys' Club at your work is to find yourself a male mentor. While most people would advise young females to seek other females as mentors, I tend to advise the opposite. In fact, if you are a black female, I advise you to seek a white male as a mentor. Why? A cross gender and cross racial mentorship relationship allows for an environment where diverse perspectives, values and ideas are valued and leveraged, not just tolerated, and one where everyone (including women, and particularly black women) can become insiders. Being a man's mentee creates an opportunity for them to recognize your potential. This makes it easy for them to allow you into their corner and create opportunities for you.

You could also break into the Old Boys' Club at work by learning how to communicate like the boys. While I urge women to not lose their natural leadership style and their sense of self, when it comes to communication style, I advise a slight shift in gear towards how men do it. I urge you not to be afraid to speak for fear that you may not be heard, because *"when we speak we are afraid our words will not be heard or welcomed. But when we are silent, we are still afraid. So it is better to speak."* (Audre Lorde). Michelle Obama once said: *"You can't make decisions based on fear and the possibility of what might happen."*

Do not seek approval when you have a case to make. Never use phrases like "I may be wrong, but I think...." Or "Am I making any sense?" Cut to the chase and make your point with confidence. If you are interrupted, say, "I'd like to finish with the point I am making first. I will come to that later." Do not succumb to the urge to lose control and get aggressive. Remember that: *"If you can speak about what you care about to a person you disagree with without denigrating or insulting them, then you may actually be heard, and you might even change their mind."* (Amy Poehler)

Being able to communicate without fear and approval from men will make men respect you for being confident and assertive. They will take you as one of their own and accept you into the Boys' Club. You will become similar to them and the "similar-to-me" syndrome will take its natural course.

To sum up this chapter: Women who find it valuable to network outside their companies should consider belonging to women-only networking clubs, where they can benefit from sharing ideas and opportunities with other women and position themselves to break into the Old Boy's Club. Those who value internal networking should rather focus on taking part in exciting projects that would add value to their departments, thus creating visibility for themselves for promotion.

8. A 'WORK-LIFE' BALANCE DOES NOT EXIST. RATHER FOCUS ON MAKING THE RIGHT WORK-LIFE CHOICES.

"There is no such thing as work-life balance. Everything worth fighting for unbalances your life." – Alain de Botton

In the movie *I Don't Know How She Does It*, Sarah Jessica Parker captures the essence of this chapter perfectly. She is a successful executive, who works in a top investment bank. She is married, with two young children, both under six years old. She finds herself battling to balance the needs of being a wife and raising young children with those of her highly demanding and stressful job. For her, every single day is a struggle. To make matters worse, while her husband understands her job demands, he disapproves of her constant absence from her family life. Her older child is not impressed either.

Traditionally, women have a greater responsibility than men in taking care of the family. A lot has been written about how women should maintain work-life balance by learning to say no, prioritising their family and establishing the correct support structures. My question, though, is: Is there even such a thing as a work-life balance, and if there is, how does it help women in accessing C-Suite positions?

Fitzsimmons, Callan et al. (2014) found that the reasons why men advance easily and faster into the C-Suite is that male CEOs have wives who could take primary responsibility for the care of their children and other domestic responsibilities. The male CEOs said that their careers had been their primary focus during the years their children were growing up and that having children did little to interrupt to their careers. They said that they managed to push their careers, as their wives had shouldered most of the domestic "burdens".

In an effort to rectify these domestic "burdens" (an implied synonym for new-born babies) for women, may governments and organizations are now focusing on creating a "work-life balance" for women. For example, the British government has introduced brand new legislation that allows parents to share maternity leave as they see fit. Mothers and fathers can now share a full thirty-seven weeks paid maternity leave. Prior to this new law, which came into effect on 1 December 2014, dads got just two unpaid weeks off.

Global health care company Roche has also made an effort to create work-life balance by introducing a unique, flexible work program which offers employees twelve days of remote work per quarter, which comes to forty-eight days a year. If an employee needs to stay at home to be with kids or sick parents or to focus on a specific project, the company trusts that they will still get their work done (Stuckey 2014). Vodafone, also in an effort to assist women achieve a better work-life balance, introduced more generous maternity leave benefits. By the end of the year, new mothers across all the countries in which Vodafone operates will qualify for four to six months fully paid maternity leave (SA Labour Law requires three months fully paid maternity leave). In addition, during the first six months of returning to work, new mothers will be allowed to work for thirty hours a week and still be paid for a forty-hour week.

Pharmaceutical company Eli Lilly offers after school programs beyond day care so children can attend science camps, math sessions, and other activities in the evening. These innovative programs enable employees with families to retain demanding positions without the worry of leaving children at home, which helps to reduce the choice women often must make between family and work (Stuckey 2014).

It is great that these companies are offering great benefits for women. But they should not offer them in an effort to create a "work-life balance". This is because a work- life balance does not exist. It is a fallacy. Once you have children, you cannot really find a balance between building a career into top management and raising them. My belief is that having children will always throw you off-balance and impact on your career building efforts. Sheryl Sandberg summed this nicely when she said, "There's no such thing as work-life balance. There's work, there's life, and there is no balance."

Working women can only achieve balance by consciously designing their lives in accordance with their top priorities. They need to have a clear understanding of what it would take for them to be successful in life, according to their own definitions of success. What is considered success by Thulisile, might be different from what success is for Neo.

For example, a woman whose top priority is to have children and spend time with them might opt to take extended maternity leave and work flexi-hours when she returns to work. She would make this choice with a full understanding that it would slow her rise through the ranks. On the other hand, a woman whose top priority is to advance rapidly into top management, would be willing to sacrifice being on top of every detail as a mother in order to put more time into her career.

In a nutshell, what I am saying is that women can have a family and build a career, but not simultaneously. You will either have to sacrifice leisure activities so you can make the most of a career opportunity, or accept slower progress up the management ladder to spend more time with your family. Trade-offs need to be made about which needs to come first. Luckily, there are options available. There are ways for women to manage the need to have a career and still have children, without the two conflicting with each other.

One way is the Apple and Facebook way. Both companies have created a new perk that gives young women employees an opportunity to build their careers in their earlier years, and have children at a later stage, when their careers are well established. The tech companies are offering to freeze eggs for female employees, so that they can use them later in their careers to have babies. There is a dearth of senior women in Silicon Valley so the perks offered by Apple and Facebook could be seen as an attempt to rectify the gender imbalance and accelerate access to top positions (Tran 2014).

Another way, which might be the best thing that companies can do to get women into top management and keep them there, is to focus more on creating leadership opportunities for them. Stuckey (2014) cites a case of one multinational oil company, which maps careers out for its employees after their first year at the company, and the career direction is adjusted yearly. Development plans, stretch assignments, promotions and networking opportunities are equal for men and women who have been rated with similar capabilities. This structure removes the chances of women not being aware of opportunities for their development at higher levels, and it creates visibility to top leadership.

Since this development program starts when they are hired, women are an equal partner in opting in or out for additional advancement for their career track. Annual reviews are used by the Talent Development team to ensure women are recognized by leadership and for selection in highly visible programs. This, for me, is what would work in getting women to the top and keeping them there, not extended maternity benefits.

THIS IS HOW WE DO

As seen in the movie cited earlier, work-life balance does not exist.

Women need to make choices based on what they believe will work for them. Jack Welch said: **"There is no such thing as work-life balance. There are work-life choices that have consequences you need to accept."** These choices include decisions about when to have children and when to build a career. My research showed that there are only two choices really.

One option is to consider having children at a young age, earlier on in your career, so that by the time you approach senior roles, your children are already in high school, at university or have left home. This way, you will have more time to acquire the necessary capital that is required to get into top management, as there would be no role conflict. This is what most of my respondents did. Most of their children are in high school or in university. Some even have children that are graduates and are working already.

Another option is to consider having children at a later stage, when you have reached the top management level that you want. One of my respondents is forty-two and has young children aged three and four. If your company offers no egg- freezing perks, take up the offer.

If you are reading this book and are thinking "Damn, these two options will not work for me. I am already in senior management and I am expecting a baby", well, there is something you can do to still position yourself for that top role that you need. You could **consider taking very little time away for maternity leave, especially when there are tight deadlines.** In my study, time taken away for maternity leave varied between as little as three weeks to four months. Consider what some of my respondents said:

"I have been on maternity leave twice and both times it was a maximum of three weeks. The second time it was just before 2010 the World Cup, and I had to get back to the office early as I was having meetings at my house, taking calls etc. Basically, there was no maternity leave. I decided to get back to the office and my bosses were relieved. I could have stayed away for four months, but it did not make sense to do that based on the amount of work that had to be done and the enormity of the project that was I was leading." (Marketing Director of a large broadcasting firm)

Remember, though, to make up for time lost with the new baby at a later stage, when things are quieter in the office. If you made a sacrifice for a bigger project earlier on, you are in a better position to make trade-offs with your boss. More often than not, bosses will even offer you more time than you deserve. One of my respondents said: *'With my two kids, I only took six weeks and five weeks maternity leave. But last year I took a the month sabbatical"* and the other said: *"I have been on maternity leave twice. The second time I went back to work after two or three weeks but I only worked two days per week for a year."*

If you work for Vodafone or one of those companies that offer generous maternity leave benefits, you may be thinking, "Liz is mad. How can she suggest that I forfeit my extended maternity leave benefit and rather choose to cut it short in favour of work?" Well, don't shoot me. I am just saying that in life there are choices. You either choose to accelerate you way to the C-Suite or to enjoy a nine-month maternity leave. You cannot have both. As Richard Matherson said:

"A man had a choice, after all. He devoted his life to his work or to his wife and children and home. It could not be combined; not in this day and age."

9. BE AWARE OF MEN'S PERCEPTIONS AND GENDER STEREOTYPES

Long-held stereotypes about the relative strengths of men and women exist. According to Kark, Waismel-Manor et al. (2012), all social interactions around management are influenced by gendered expectations and associations. Antal and Izraeli (1993), point to a specific, persistent stereotype that associates management with being male. In other words, leadership and management connote "male". Schein, Müller et al. (1996) beautifully summed up this perception as "Think Manager, Think Male" (TMTM).

One significant factor affecting women's ability to reach top management is the limited engagement and support of men. A Mckinsey (2014) report found that generally men are less likely than women to see value in diversity initiatives and more likely to believe that too many measures supporting women are unfair to men. This report found that while nearly all male and female executives express some level of agreement that women can lead as effectively as men do, male respondents are not as convinced.

In other words, men do not se why they should support women to get into top management. This can be explained by a role congruity theory of prejudice toward female leaders, which proposes that perceived incongruity between the female gender role and leadership roles leads to two forms of prejudice: (a) perceiving women less favourably than men as potential occupants of leadership roles and (b) evaluating behaviour that fulfils the prescriptions of a leader role less favourably when it is enacted by a woman (Eagly and Karau 2002).

This implies that attitudes are less positive toward female than male leaders and potential leaders and that expectations of women by male bosses are simply lower, resulting in them being overlooked for certain opportunities. Fitzsimmons, Callan et al. (2014) cite a case in point that shows that women are perceived as being incapable of being on top. They refer to two female executives who were responsible for starting up companies in which they were CEOs and listing them on the Australian stock Exchange. Once the companies were listed, the female CEOs had difficulty convincing their boards that they should remain CEOs, as their boards were concerned about investor perceptions of having a female at the helm.

As a result of these perceptions, women, particularly those who work in male-dominated industries (e. g. financial services, engineering, computer science, mining, building and construction), often struggle to figure out how to gain respect from their male counterparts. They feel intimidated and begin to question their leadership style. A McKinsey (2013) survey revealed that there are various factors hindering women's advancement into top management. But of particular importance is the perception among women that their leadership styles don't "fit" in the prevailing leadership styles.

Stereotypically, males are expected to act agentically (in their own interest) with aggression and competitiveness. Females are expected to act communally, with sensitivity (Phelan, Moss-Racusin et al. 2008). Women are associated with communal qualities, which convey a concern for the compassionate treatment of others. These qualities include being especially affectionate, helpful, friendly, kind and sympathetic, as well as interpersonally sensitive, gentle and soft-spoken. In contrast, men are associated with agentic qualities that convey assertion, forcefulness, dominance, ambition and control.

It has been argued that women's communal style enables them to be effective leaders, because as Cohen (2000) points out, effective leadership is often defined in terms of one's ability to influence a group of people towards a common goal. However, their ability to fully engage in influencing behaviour is limited by a "double bind" (Carli 2006). A double bind means that women are caught up between being feminine and masculine in their leadership style. If they are highly compassionate and sympathetic, they may be criticized for not being assertive, effective leaders. They may not be heard in meetings because, as Oakley (2000) points out, in male-dominated large corporations, their inputs and voices are often stifled.

The other side of the "double-bind" that women are faced with is that, if they are aggressive, they may be criticized for lacking compassion. Either way, women cannot win when it comes to management style. In Sotho, this phenomenon is referred to as *"Kgomo ya moshate. O a gapa, o molato. O a lesa, o molato".*

Unfortunately, current approaches towards getting women into top management focus on "fixing" them and helping them to blend in and adapt to the way men lead, rather than supporting them to speak out and find their own voice. Women are being coached and trained to act and think like men, if they are to make it in top management. Instead of being encouraged to speak in a way that depicts their actual values, they are being made to believe that it would be a career-limiting move to act like a woman. They are being coached to "think like a woman, act like a man".

Due to these challenges, Eagly and Carli (2007) find that female leaders often struggle to cultivate an appropriate and effective leadership style. They believe that in order to be accepted by their male peers, they need to adopt a style with which male (or older) managers are comfortable. As a result, women try to fit in by compromising their self-styles. For instance, they drop their natural soft, high-pitched voice, for a deeper, more masculine one. They adopt traits and attributes that do not come naturally to them and so they lose their sense of authenticity. Compromising authentic leadership is detrimental, as this is a desired and effective leadership style for top executives.

In South Africa, women's leadership style is also impacted by another kind of a "double-bind", which is embedded in African culture. This is what I call the *"bra Mike"* dilemma, whereby younger African people are expected to prefix the names of older males with bra (township slang for brother), in order to acknowledge the age gap and to show respect. This is expected even in professional environments. Older women also expect this respect from younger folks, but men are much more sensitive to it.

This presents a great dilemma for a younger female professional. If the young woman abides by cultural norms and addresses Mike as bra Mike, she risks shaking up the hierarchical protocol. The older staff might begin to take advantage of her and not take instructions from her, resulting in her being perceived as weak and unable to manage people.

On the other hand, If she refers to him as Mike, instead of bra Mike, she will be perceived as being insensitive and offensive. If she is educated in a private or model C school, she is labelled a coconut (black outside, but white inside), *"e tletseng ka lenyatso blind"* (with the highest level of disrespect). She may also be perceived to be bossy, and women are also scared to be seen as bossy as they fear being disliked. They are just preoccupied with being seen as nice. In her book, Sheryl Sandberg writes about how, as a girl, she felt ashamed when people called her bossy. She had great difficulty in taking an authoritative position, even when there was a need to. All for fear of being disliked.

Lastly, another barrier that women who want to access the C-Suite face, due to men's perceptions, is that, once they have children, they want a "work-life balance". Men (who are still decision-makers in male dominated industries) assume that women with children would rather spend more time at home with their children and, therefore, should not be bothered with offers for promotions into more challenging demanding roles. Eagly and Carli (2007) cite a male decision- maker who said that he did not want to talk about a certain woman who was a potential candidate for a promotion because she had children.

A McKinsey report (2012) also cited a male leader who said: "For one opening, we had an employee who was highly qualified – she was running operations in Asia. However, we didn't ask her if she would be interested in the position, since she was pregnant and we assumed that she wouldn't want to move."

The perception that what women with children want is work-life balance is wrong. In a report by Hewitt and Marshall (2013), women said that in order for them to succeed at work they needed five things: to feel in control of their career path, to have their work recognised, to find meaning and purpose in their work, to be able to empower others and to have financial security. Work-life balance is not on the list.

Unfortunately for young women, until decision-makers are made aware of what women want, this perception will still exist for a long time. Having children will always be associated with having no ambition to get into the highest level of the corporate ladder. Worst of all, decision makers will not make it their business to ask a woman with children what her plans are, in case they are seen to be sticking their noses where they do not belong – in the women's private lives. So, the onus is on the woman concerned to state her position.

THIS IS HOW WE DO

Find a way to navigate a "double-bind": assert yourself forcefully if it is necessary and be gentle and feminine if the situation allows.

Leadership style should be adapted to the particular demands of the situation, the particular requirements of the people involved and the particular challenges facing the organization. Always remember that *"There is no 'one' way to be a perfect leader, but there are a million ways to be a good one."* (Mark W. Boyer)

In the book *Primal Leadership*, Daniel Goleman, who popularized the notion of "Emotional Intelligence", describes six different styles of leadership – Visionary, Commanding, Democratic, Affilliative, Coaching and Pace-setting. The most effective leaders can move among these styles, adopting the one that meets the needs of the moment. They can all become part of the leader's repertoire.

A Harvard Business Review article refers to the 2012 study by The Hay Group which found that outstanding women leaders said that they navigate the double-bind by using a combination of both stereotypically masculine leadership styles (e. g., being Authoritative or Visionary) and feminine leadership styles (e. g., being more Affilliative or Participative). Consider, for example, the case of Jenna Lyons, creative Director and President of retailer J. Crew, who said: "Managing creative people – not so easy. A lot of emotion, a lot of stroking. Some people need tough love. Some people need a lot of love."

Address the 'bra Mike' dilemma by communicating with older males with respect, but firmly. It is up to you how you choose to address them, but when disciplining them for non- performance, or any other offence, be especially mindful not to use offensive body language, such as pointing a finger or raising your voice. However, be firm. It does not matter if you are twenty-nine and bra Mike is fifty-nine, *"Jobo ke Jobo"* (a job is a job), and performance is expected of everyone.

Do not engage in stereotypical behaviour. Women should not act the way men expect them to. Naturally, women are nurturing beings and this is not something they should be afraid to show in the office. The trick is to not appear too gentle and kind. "Manners are great, but politeness can stunt relationships" (Yudelowitz, Koch et al. 2002). For example, being nurturing does not mean women should always be the ones offering to bring men coffee to their desks or to clear the dirty cups in the boardroom after a meeting.

Embrace being bossy. Sandberg's book *Lean In* teaches women to be assertive at work and home, and to view bossiness as a virtue and not a flaw. Bossiness is actually a great leadership trait. *"I just love bossy women. I could be around them all day. To me, bossy is not a pejorative term at all. It means somebody's passionate and engaged and ambitious and doesn't mind leading."* Amy Poehler

Lastly, be sure to let your bosses know about your ambitions to rise into top management. If you make it clear to the decision makers that having children does not mean that you want to leave work at 3pm to spend time with them, instead of working on an important high-profile project, they will know where you stand. You will be positioning yourself for that promotion that you want.

10. CONSIDERING A CAREER GAP? THINK TWICE BEFORE YOU ROLL THOSE DICE

When I was in my postgraduate year of study in 1994, I remember a female professor introducing herself on the first day of class and telling us that she had been on sabbatical for the previous five years. She explained that she needed some time off, as she had been teaching for more than a decade, without a break. I thought to myself, "Cool, so women can just decide to take a career break for half a decade and just resume from where they left off when they were ready for a come back".

It appears that I was naïve to think that this is the case across all sectors. The concept of a career break seemed to work in academia, but not quite in the corporate world. Perhaps this could be explained by the shortage of female professors in South Africa, which is still the case twenty-one years on.

Of course, there are women in the corporate sector who have taken long breaks from their careers to raise their children, start their own businesses or simply just to recollect themselves and reflect on their lives. Even in my study, there were such women. These women have managed to come back into top management positions and to pick up from where they left off. It may have taken them longer than the average period to secure the corporate jobs that they sought, but they eventually succeeded.

However, there are few such women. In my research, less than 10% of my respondents took long breaks and got away with it. The rest never even tried as they have learned that, unless you possess a skill that is critical to the economy and is only possessed by fewer than 1% of the population, taking a career break for longer than six months is a gamble. It could be a career-limiting move. In fact, in might even translate into career suicide. Here is why:

Firstly, research has shown that social capital, the ability to create professional groups that are influential in one's business environment and to network with such groups, is critical in accessing C-Suite positions. In addition, Fitzsimmons, Callan et al (2014) argue that it is not just any form of capital that is required. Rather, it is a certain volume and structure of social capital that is required.

The authors maintain that the difference in the volume and structure of capital relate to women's ability to maintain continuous service in one organization, compared to men. Often, after taking time away from work for reasons such as maternity leave or to look after a sick parent or child, in many instances females change their role or seek a new position in a new firm, usually outside the industry in which they worked prior to having a child. This greatly affects the social capital and networks that the women would have built prior to having a child. As a result, their chances of advancing to top management are affected.

Secondly, a US study on unemployment found that managers prefer to hire a less qualified candidate over one who has been out of work for more than six months. They assume that a career gap has resulted in the deterioration of skills (Miles 2015). In other words, employers consider candidates who have been away from work for six months or longer to be stale and irrelevant.

Those who seek work after having been out of corporate life for over ten years (or return soldiers, as I call them) are considered to be more out of tune, as their skills have "expired". Their talents are perceived to have simply reached their sell-by date. Even when they know that they have reached their sell-by date, some women still attempt to get back into top management roles, as they believe that they have still not reached their use-by date (the latter date always comes before the former, check the cheese in your fridge).

Unfortunately, return soldiers are often confronted with the unconscious bias of gender, age and lack of recent experience. Despite their enviable qualifications and great track records, they are often discriminated against in favour of younger candidates with more recent qualifications. They too often are tarred with the "homemaker" stereotype, assumed to be unambitious, low in self-confidence and inflexible. Even enlightened employers ask us whether all returners want to work part-time. As many are over forty- five years old, they can also be perceived as technological dinosaurs and slow learners. One ex-finance director was told she would not be able to "jump back onto the corporate fast train" (Miles 2015)

I have personally experienced the plight of the return soldier. Some ten years ago, I, together with my husband, left the corporate world to run two Woolworths (Marks and Spencer in the UK) franchised stores, as franchisees. We left our comfortable corporate jobs and went on to set up the stores from scratch and to run the businesses successfully. We established ourselves as entrepreneurs to be reckoned with. We exceeded the targets that were set out in the feasibility studies for both stores and, as a result, we would often be singled out as a success story at franchisee conferences, which was a bit embarrassing.

Unfortunately, seven years later, Woolworths decided to de-franchise and convert all franchised stores into corporate stores. My husband, with his large appetite for retailing, went on to acquire another franchised retailing business. I had had enough of the retailing trading hours and wanted out. So, I immediately updated my CV with the entrepreneurial bit, which I hoped would demonstrate to potential employers that I can set up and run an enterprise of my own and run it profitably, a skill that is also crucial in the corporate world.

I was in for a big surprise. Even with post-graduate qualifications, my impressive CV and a great track record in marketing in some of the world's largest multinational FMCG companies, including Unilever, Coca-Cola and SC Johnson, it was hard to get back into the corporate world. Although no potential employer had provided me with honest feedback, I knew that I was potentially perceived to be a technological dinosaur, who had reached a sell by date and needed to give younger people with more recent qualification a chance. I was discriminated against based on my age (though I was still under forty) and the long corporate gap that I had taken. In some countries, the plight of return soldiers has not gone unnoticed and some measures are being taken to address it. In the UK, investment banks have taken the lead in changing business's attitudes to women returners through the development of "returnships". They have put together programs that have demonstrated that talented women are perfectly capable of coming back into senior jobs in the most demanding corporate environments. However, not much

progress has been made in this regard.

In an effort to create employment and reduce the plight of people without jobs, in 2011 President Barack Obama proposed a Bill that included banning discrimination against jobless people. Was this Bill passed into law? You guessed it. No. It was not. Congress did not show any interest in the matter.

In South Africa, the silent barriers facing return soldiers have not even been acknowledged as an issue. They have never even made it onto the parliamentary agenda as a matter for discussion. It is one of those issues that everyone know about and acknowledges is wrong and unfair, but it is only spoken about quietly down the corridors. Until Julius Malema or Floyd Shivambu of the EFF party make it an issue, it will remain a non-issue.

THIS IS HOW WE DO...

Think twice before you decided to take a temporary break to run your own business, travel, raise kids or any other reason. If you do take a break, make it very short or risk being a return soldier. In fact, my advice is: never take any long-term break, unless it is absolutely necessary.

11. WATCH OUT FOR THE ELEPHANT IN THE ROOM, WEARING HIGH HEELS AND LIPSTICK

As I have alluded to in the chapter about women's leadership style, and as research has shown, women are generally the more empathetic sex and are by nature more attuned to their own and others' feelings. However, when it comes to treating each other, women often find it difficult to display these qualities. I am not saying that women are always horrible to one another. Not all women are like that. But we would be fooling ourselves if we fail to acknowledge that women can be their worst enemies at work. Ever watched the movie *Mean Girls*? If you have, you will know what this chapter is all about. If you think bullying only happens at schools, think again. Workplace bullying does happen, and in most cases where women are victims, the perpetrators are women. These perpetrators make it their mission to make other women's lives at work a misery. While other women innocently plan their workday and pen down their to-do list, these "ugly" women are planning a hit list. They are writing down names of whom the recipients of their verbal abuse and performance sabotage are going to be for the day/week/ month.

A study by the Workplace Bullying Institute (bullyinginstitute.org), which examined office behaviour like verbal abuse, job sabotage, misuse of authority and destroying of relationships, found that female bullies aim at other women more than 70% of the time. Bullies who are men, by contrast, tend to be equal-opportunity tormentors when it comes to the gender of their target. They lash out at women as much as they do at men.

Both men and women are equally susceptible to overwhelming emotions of jealousy of their more successful colleagues. However, men often handle their feelings of envy and jealousy with humour and a left-handed compliment. For example, a man might say: "I'm going to whip your butt on our sales goals this month." Women, on the other hand, adopt a more vicious response. It is not uncommon for a newly-promoted women to hear this remark from a female colleague: "Who did you sleep with for the promotion?"

Female managers are also faced with the challenge of the PHD syndrome. No. This is not a situation where all the women in your department obtain doctoral degrees, with the aim of making you feel under-qualified. It is an acronym for a syndrome known as the Pull Her Down syndrome. In a case where it is the boss that engages in the same behaviour towards her female subordinate, the syndrome is know as the "set-up-to fail' syndrome. This is where a boss, out of fear of competition from a newly-promoted female manager, makes statements such as, "I know I've been working with her for only a month, but I have feeling that the wrong person was promoted". This is where the boss gives you a tough project without the right support, advice and tools to implement it.

Bosses might also engage in behaviour that they may deem harmless, but that may be uncomfortable to their subordinates. We spoke earlier about how women need to differentiate themselves from the pack by finding their own USP. Throughput my career, my USP was my dress code. I was well known as the lady in Marketing who wore power suits and designer shirts, even on casual Fridays. Even during my MBA, I would rock a suit and heels to class, particularly when I had a syndicate presentation to do. Lecturers and fellow candidates would ask if I had an interview. That was just me.

I once had a female boss who seemed to be annoyed by my power dressing. I occupied the first office in the corridor, after the staircase landing. My boss made it a point that each day, before she got into her office, to come into my office and say, "What are you wearing today? Turn around and let's see. Miss South Africa. Miss Money." While this might have seemed like an innocent behaviour, it was annoying to me. Call me over-sensitive, but I found this to be a subtle form of bullying. It had a malicious undertone to it.

But that was not the worst thing that the same boss did to me. When I'd been in that company for about two weeks, the regional directors from the US headquarters were due to visit our SA office in a week's time. The marketing team representing the various brands had to go onto a common mainframe to input performance and projects on their various brands. I accidentally deleted all the info on the mainframe, instead of just deleting a small portion on my brands. The boss lady knew what to do to help me to rectify the mistake, but she chose to press the alarm to alert everyone that their info on the mainframe had gone. I became known as the "mainframe killer".

But why would some women go on to deliberately hurt and ruin the reputation of other women? In her articled titled *A sisterhood of Workplace Infighting*, Klaus (2009) states that the most popular one is the scarcity excuse – the idea that there are too few spots at the top, so women at more senior levels are unwilling to assist female colleagues who could potentially replace them.

"Many women who have attained a certain career level don't want to see others potentially competing with them. They want to remain the queen bees. That's a great folly in our society." (Dolly Mokgatle) Instead of pulling more women to the top in order to close the gender gap, some women executives feel that no other women should sit next to them in the boardroom.

Another explanation is what Klaus call the "D. I. Y. Bootstrap Theory", which goes like this: "If I had to pull myself up by the bootstraps to get ahead with no one to help me, why should I help you? Do it yourself!" This may be the case with older women who entered top management when things were particularly difficult for women, such as during the glass-ceiling period. Often, these sentiments would be echoed by women who were "the first woman to....", "the first black woman to..." or "the youngest woman to ever...". They want to be referred to as the only woman in top management in that organization, for as long as possible.

Women may also be horrible to other women because they are worried about showing favouritism toward those other women, so instead they can end up going too far in the other direction and go out of their way to not help their female colleagues. Most women executives know this scenario too well. When a young women is promoted into an executive position, the female executive that had been there for longer might feel that she should not be seen to be soft towards her by her male colleagues. As a result, she may become unfriendly, cold or horrible towards the newer executive.

Andthenthere'stheideathatsomewomentakechallenges or criticism personally, hold grudges or get caught up in petty arguments. As a result, they take out their frustrations by venting out on other women. Having problems at home, while things seem to be going well for other women at home, might also cause jealousy in some women. Competition, jealousy and envy might breed wrath towards fellow women. While men also compete and become envious of one another's positive achievements, they hardly make it their personal mission to make fellow men go through pain and hurt.

THIS IS HOW WE DO

Lobby for the support of male colleagues, especially your male superiors. Make sure that your male bosses are always ready to defend why you are in the position that you are in. If these men publicly defend your skills and expertise, the bullies are likely to back off.

In the "mainframe killer" case, my boss had been impressed by how I had presented myself to the panel at the interview. As part of the selection process, I was given a case study to work on and to present my ideas to the board, which was all male. The board was very impressed with how I had carried out the presentation and how fresh my ideas were. I had immediately created visibility for myself, before I even started working there. So, while my female boss exposed the mainframe thing as a huge scandal, they just saw it as an honest mistake. My boss told my colleagues that I made a mistake, which IT would be able to sort out, and that we should just move on.

Find a wing-woman. Look for a woman in another department who is as ambitious as you, is trustworthy but is not vying for the same job that you are. Work as a team and make it your mission to trumpet each other's success to right people. If it is someone else who is trumpeting your achievements (another woman), the "ugly" women will see no point in continuing to harass you. At this company, my wing-woman was also in Marketing, but she was looking after the West African market and she was senior to me. She also down played the mainframe issue and told everyone it was a genuine mistake. After only a few hours, the whole hullabaloo quietened down.

Do not suck up. Most women react to bullies by sucking up to them, with the hope that they will get off their case and leave them in peace. They offer to side with them in meetings, even when they know the bully is talking rubbish, hold the lift for the bully even when she is still in the bathroom or offer their sandwich at lunch, even when they know they are starving to the point of shaking. Show the bullies that you deserve to be where you are by continuing to do the best you can.

While it is not always wise to involve yourself in things that do not concern you, as a woman you should have the courage to call on colleagues if they are treating other female workers unfairly.

I sum up the chapter with the words of Klaus (2009): "If we really want to clear one of the last remaining hurdles to gender parity and career success, let's start treating one another not worse or better, but simply as well as we already treat the guys — or better yet, the way we want our nieces, daughters, granddaughters and sisters to be treated"

12. FROM MANAGEMENT TO LEADERSHIP

OK. So you now know about the obstacles that women who want to enter the C-Suite are faced with and what other women have done to navigate them and get through to the top. By now, you should be thinking, "I can do this! Now that I know what challenges I may be faced with and how others have worked through them, I know what to do. It looks tough, but I am ready to be the next Chief.........Officer."

So, you do want to be the next CEO, CFO, COO, CMO, CRO or CCO? You want to be a member of the C-Suite? That's great! Ambition is great. And besides, why not? I have pointed out before that South Africa's EXCOs and boardrooms are waiting to welcome you. There are opportunities galore for young and upcoming women executives. Your time is now.

But let me ask you one question. Why do you want to be in the C-Suite? I don't know your motivation but I have an idea. It is because we envy our current role models who occupy those positions. We aspire to have the money, power, status, control and prestige that come with C-Suite titles. We want the executive SUV and the big corner office with automated blinds, with a view over the Sandton skyline, or Atlantic ocean. We want journalists to trip over themselves trying to get us on the cover of the glossy business magazines or luxurious television studios.

Of course all of these sound great, as they bring the ultimate recognition and confirmation of the fact that we have arrived. But this is not what true leadership is about. Anybody can get filthy rich quite easily.

Leadership, though, is not easy. Ask any business leader. It can be very lonely up there. You may find yourself torn, disillusioned and powerless, if you do not possess the right leadership skills.

The next chapters do not have a 'This is How we Do" section at the end. Unlike the previous chapters, they are not based on the experiences of other women. They are simply bonus chapters that are geared towards teaching you some of the greatest leadership skills. Yes. You do need to learn leadership, because *"No great manager or leader ever fell from heaven, it's learned not inherited."* (Tom Northup)

"You have to do your own growing no matter how tall your grandfather was." (Abraham Lincoln)

13. THINK AND ACT LIKE A LEADER BEFORE YOU EVEN BECOME ONE

"You don't have to hold a position, in order to be a leader." Henry
Ford

In order to achieve top executive positions, women need to demonstrate a deep understanding of the personal and organizational leadership traits that are required to solve today's complex business challenges.

First, they need to understand the difference between management and leadership because being a great manager, with the greatest technical expertise, is not enough to make one a great leader. Although they go hand in hand and complement each other, leadership and management are not the same thing. Leadership goals go beyond management. Leadership, instead of management, is necessary for outcomes that exceed expectations.

So what is the difference between management and leadership? The short version of the answer to this question is: The manager's job is to plan, organize and coordinate. The leader's job is to inspire and motivate. The long version of the answer is "leadership is purpose driven action that brings about change or transformation based on values ideals, vision, symbols and emotional exchanges. Management is objectives-driven, resulting in stability, grounded in rationality, bureaucratic means and the fulfilment of contractual obligations (i. e. transactions)." (Day and Antonakis 2012).

Warren Bennis, in his 1989 book titled *On becoming a leader*, has compiled a list of differences between a manager and a leader. Key differences include: the manager administers, the leader innovates; the manager relies on control, the leader inspires trust; the manager has a short- range view, the leader has a long-range perspective; the manager has his or her eye always on the bottom line, the leader's eye is on the horizon; the manager focuses on systems and structure, the leader focuses on people.

There was a time when management and leadership could be separated. For example, in a factory, a supervisor was responsible for following orders from his boss, doing the staff scheduling and making sure that the staff pitch up to work, sign the attendance register and perform the tasks he allocates to them. Today, however, as management guru, Peter Drucker points out, the task is to lead people.

But why are people a key focus of leadership? Should we rather not focus on the processes, structures and policies that are surely guaranteed to generate profit for the shareholders? Is that not what business is about, in the first place? Why do people matter?

Today, with the advent of globalization, the external environment in which businesses operate is characterized by constant change. It is this change that threatens the sustainability of enterprises. With change, comes discomfort and resistance. Change is meant to bring progress, but for some reason, people appreciate progress but not change. Mark Twain said: *"I'm all for progress. It's change I don't like."* This is where leadership comes in. "The point of leadership is to initiate change and make it feel like progress" (Yudelowitz, Koch et al. 2002). It is about making people like the unlikable. Harry Truman summed it up nicely when he said: "Leadership is the ability to get men to do what they don't like to do, and like it". If it is effective, leadership persuades people who would otherwise carry on doing what they are doing, to do something different, in accordance with a shared view of what that "something different" comprises.

Leadership uses change, to make progress (Yudelowitz, Koch et al. 2002).

In other words, leadership is about moving people from a present that they know and are comfortable with, to a future that they do not know but will benefit greatly from. How does one move people forward, from the present to the future? More importantly, what kinds of people are able to influence others to see things their way, and move forward with them?

In short, what makes a great leader in today's economy? What should young women be aware of and work on, in order to develop themselves into leaders? The answers lie in the next chapters.

Here is a quick word of caution, before we delve deeper into leadership development. Firstly, let me remind you that this book is about business leadership, not leadership in general. Business leadership is effective and profitable adaptation to the conditions around the organization; it is about choices and actions that are mindful sensible and yet courageous too. Taking and executing decisions in a way that is responsive and flexible, as well as deliberate and influential, that makes sense to colleagues, and gains commitment form them (Yudelowitz, Koch et al. 2002).

Secondly, be aware that developing your leadership skills will not happen overnight. This is a process that will only be beneficial if you work on it one step at a time. If you put yourself under pressure to become a leader overnight, you might suffer from the Boiling Frog Syndrome. It is said that if one drops a frog into a pot of boiling water, it will jump out due to its instinctive defence mechanism. But if one places a frog in a pot of cool water and gradually increases the temperature, the frog will sit

85

in the water until it is boiled!

If you are too hard on yourself, you may find the whole thing overwhelming and give up too soon. Slow adjustments are acceptable on the way to a major change, but the same change made dramatically is not tolerated. So do work on your future, but take the future in small doses.

14. AUTHENTIC LEADERSHIP

The 21st century has brought with it many challenges for business, including a leadership crisis. Leading in a complex environment and the pressure for creating profit for shareholders has driven leaders towards unethical and corrupt behaviour. There is an urgent need for leaders who lead with purpose, value and integrity and who are good stewards of the legacy they inherited from their predecessors.   We need a new kind of leader – the authentic leader – to take us out of the current leadership crisis (George 2003).

That is why authenticity is a hot topic in business and leadership today. Authenticity is about being ethical. It is about a leader's level of moral development and his or her ability and willingness to stand by his or her core values. Authenticity is not a trait. It is not an innate attribute that one possesses, like charm, friendliness or aggression. It is a condition, or a state of balance. To remain authentic, one needs to constantly review endure that with every circumstances, their values and behaviours are in sync.

Authenticity is an important component of leadership development. Living a life strongly connected to your belief system promotes growth, learning and psychological well being. Individual authenticity is important for organizations as well. People who are authentic bring their whole selves to their jobs and participate fully and honestly in the workplace (Ruderman and Ragolsky 2014).

While authenticity is increasingly becoming an essential element of leadership for both men and women, it seems to worry women more than it does men. Today's business is characterisedbyconstantchangeintheexternalenvironment, which forces companies to continuously realign structures, hierarchies, tasks, goals and strategies. Any major change, such as a re-structuring and retrenchments, might bring women face-to-face with issues of authenticity.

Moreover, most organizations have a culture of placing a premium on conformity at the expense of authenticity. This requires that women, particularly those working in male-dominated industries or organizations, suppress their personal style. As a result, female managers tend to put on a false front, compromising their true values and what they stand for. They find it difficult to achieve a healthy alignment between their values and behaviour.

When women feel the need to restrain their personal style to fit in with the prevailing organizational culture, their authenticity suffers. It is difficult to develop your capabilities when you are suppressing your true values and style or are distracted by inner conflict (Ruderman and Ragolsky 2014). As they struggle with feelings of inauthenticity, women's energies become drained. They lose interest in their work and, in most cases, they leave the organizations.

In a 2014 study by the Centre for Creative Leadership, one study participant had worked for the same company for more than fifteen years. Sophie had steadily advanced in her organization and truly liked her job. When her department got a new boss, however, everything changed. His approach was completely different from that of her previous bosses, and it made Sophie uncomfortable. At first she told herself that he simply had a distinctive style, but it soon became evident that his tactics and ways of handling business issues lacked integrity, ethics, and even morals. He had no qualms about misleading people and pursuing hidden agendas.

Sophie could no longer reconcile her job with her values. She felt dishonest and without control over her own life. Her performance and well-being declined. Sophie decided the only way to fix the situation was to leave it. When a company job opened up in a different city, she jumped at the opportunity. Now she is thriving as a manager in the new location, where the business practices align with her values and allow her to work with integrity (Ruderman and Ragolsky 2014).

Women should realise that while managers are assessed on performance and technical know-how, leaders are assessed on authenticity. To position yourself as a great future leader, you need to start working on issues of ethics, integrity and honesty.

"Presenting leadership as a list of carefully defined qualities (like strategic, analytical and performance-oriented) no longer holds. Instead, true leadership stems from individuality that is honestly and sometimes imperfectly expressed... Leaders should strive for authenticity over perfection." (Sheryl Sandberg)

15. EMOTIONAL INTELLIGENCE (EQ)

Ever wondered why the big boss has decided to promote Thembi instead of Thandi, while both women have a BSc. Computer Science from reputable universities, were recruited into the company at the same time and have been performing the same duties? No, it is not because Thandi has a weave and the boss prefers Thembi's dreadlocks. It is neither about the fact that Thembi's IQ score came out higher than Thandi's. It is because Thembi has been consistently displaying leadership qualities and companies prefer to promote leaders.

Don't get me wrong. There is nothing wrong with Thembi having a higher IQ, but that does not count much for the big bosses when they decided who to promote. As Bennis, Cherniss et al. (2003) put it, intellect still matters, certainly. You generally need a certain number of IQ points just to get in the game. But management guru Daniel Goleman's great contribution has been to make clear the astonishing degree to which, once you're in the game, becoming a star is largely attributable to factors beyond intellect — factors such as maturity, emotional health, and grownup-ness. These factors can be summed up as Emotional Intelligence. Emotional intelligence (EI), according to Goleman, is linked to abilities that involve skill in managing emotion in oneself and others and that are predictive of superior performance in work roles. It, at the most general level, refers to the *abilities to recognize and regulate emotions in ourselves and in others.* Emotional Intelligence has four major components: Self-

Awareness, Self-Management, Social Awareness, and Relationship Management.

The first component of emotional intelligence is emotional self-awareness, knowing what one feels. Self-awareness has been argued to be one of the biggest contributing factors to effective leadership and, for this reason, I have dedicated a whole section to it in the next chapter.

The second component of EQ, emotional self-management, is the ability to regulate distressing affects like anxiety and anger and to inhibit emotional impulsivity.

This component of EQ encompasses six competencies. First on the list is the emotional self-control competence, which manifests largely as the absence of distress and disruptive feelings. Signs of this competence include being unfazed in stressful situations or dealing with a hostile person without lashing out in return.

Imagine that one of your employees has been disgruntled with you for a while and instead of telling you her reasons, she prefers to speak about in the corridors with colleagues, behind your back. The only sign of unhappiness you are able to pick up his her poor performance and bad attitude towards you. One morning she shows up in your office with a winning lotto ticket in one hand and a resignation letter in another. She tells you what an awful manager and loser you are. She spits on your desk and says, "Goodbye, witch".

Any other manager would jump onto this woman and attempt to take her eyeballs out. The first words that might come out of her mouth would be, "You, non-performing b*tch. Get the hell out of my office." But a manager with self-control abilities will be able to tap into their anger-management competencies, remain calm and say: "Congratulations on winning the lotto. Thank you for having been in our team. Good luck with your new venture and God bless!"

The second competence of self-management is trustworthiness, which is all about letting others know your values and principles, intentions and feelings, and acting in ways that are consistent with them. Trustworthy individuals are forthright about their own mistakes and confront others about their lapses. A deficit in this ability operates as a career derailer (Goleman, 1998b).

I once had a boss who would address us, all his managers, as a group and make certain commitments and promises to all of us, only to say something else later. For example, at some stage our company was going through a re-structuring and there were going to be retrenchments. He assured all of us that we would not be affected. Later that week, we went out to a Christmas party for our division. The other people from my department did not attend. Only myself, my boss and my subordinate made it. My boss said in a low voice: "Between the three of us, you two are the only ones in my department who will get to keep your jobs. The rest are on their way out." Needless to say, I immediately lost all the respect I had for him.

In another company, a woman was hired into a senior marketing role. After a few weeks, everyone started to notice a bump on her tummy, which she said nothing about. After just four months of being with the company, she went on maternity leave. In her absence, the head of our department (a man) and HR Manager (a woman), would make utterances in the corridors, such as "Can you believe it? She fooled all of us in the interview. She was five months pregnant and she said nothing about it. What a snake!" In her presence, they would smile at her and pretend that they did not know about the pregnancy. I resented them for this and lost respect for them too. They were the actual snakes.

Conscientiousness is the third competence of self- management. It is about being careful, self – disciplined and scrupulous in attending to responsibilities. It is about keeping things running as they should, by being energetic and action-oriented. It is one thing for a senior manager to, once in a while, ask her subordinate to urgently attend a meeting on her behalf as something has come up, but it is another thing completely if something comes up all the time and the subordinate always has to carry all the responsibilities of her boss. Good leaders take their responsibilities and job performance seriously. *"The prize of responsibility is greatness." (Winston Churchill)*

Adaptability, the fourth component of self-management, is perhaps the most critical component of leading in today's business environment. Nowadays, business is constantly being affected by the external environment, forever causing leaders to adapt their strategies. The age-old adage of "Adapt or Die" has never been more relevant.

In the face of dynamic change, leaders need to remain comfortable with the anxiety that often accompanies uncertainty and to think "out of the box", displaying on-the- job creativity and applying new ideas to achieve results. Conversely, people who are uncomfortable with risk and change become naysayers who can undermine innovative ideas or be slow to respond to a shift in the marketplace.

A recent case in point here is Nokia, which was once the number one handset brand in South Africa. Nokia lost that position because they failed to recognise the external changing environment, which was then moving towards smartphones. Blackberry, a new entrant in the market, realised that opportunity and grabbed it, becoming the Number 1 smartphone brand in the country. However, Blackberry became inflexible to the shifting market demands and stopped being innovative. They were overtaken by Apple's iPhone and Samsung smartphones. Businesses with less formal and more ambiguous, autonomous and flexible roles for employees open flows of information, and multidisciplinary, team-oriented structures experience greater innovation (Bennis, Cherniss et al. 2003).

The fifth competence of self-management is Initiative. It is an ability act before being forced to do so by external events.
This often means taking anticipatory action to avoid problems before they happen or taking advantage of opportunities before they are

visible to anyone else. Individuals who lack initiative are reactive rather than proactive, lacking the farsightedness that can make the critical difference between a wise decision and a poor one. "Without initiative, leaders are simply workers in leadership positions." Bo Benett.

Social Awareness is the third element of Emotional Intelligence. It manifests in three competencies, including empathy. Empathy does not mean adopting other people's emotions as one's own and trying to please everybody. Rather, empathy means thoughtfully considering employees' feelings – along with other factors – in the process of making intelligent decisions. Sensitivity to others is critical for superior job performance whenever the focus is on interactions with people.

Empathy plays a key role in the retention of talent, particularly in today's information economy. Leaders have always needed empathy to develop and keep good people, but today the stakes are higher. When good people leave, they take the company's knowledge with them. Consider, for example, the case of the boss of a large talk radio station in Johannesburg. When she realised that one of her most valued employees was facing the challenges of leaving her new-born baby at home, she allowed the employee to bring the baby to work with her.

Social awareness also plays a key role in the service competence, the ability to identify a client's or customer's often unstated needs and concerns and then match them to products or services; this empathic strategy distinguishes star sales performers from average ones. It also means taking a long-term perspective, sometimes trading off immediate gains in order to preserve customer relationships (Bennis, Cherniss et al. 2003).

Building trusting relationships is a cluster that addresses our abilities to trust ourselves, trust others, and allow the creative discord that results in sound, effective solutions. These abilities can enhance interactions with customers, clients and work teams. They can also save time and help us get things done at a more substantive, meaningful level.

Effective managers are those who are able to attune themselves to or influence the emotions of another person. Goleman argues that this ability in turn builds on other domains of EQ, particularly self-management and social awareness. If we cannot control our emotional outbursts or impulses and lack empathy, there is less chance we will be effective in our relationships.

One of the key elements of relationship management is developing others, which involves sensing people's developmental needs and bolstering their abilities – a talent not just of excellent coaches and mentors, but also of outstanding leaders. Competence in developing others is a hallmark of superior managers.

Influence is another essential competence in leaders, when we handle and manage emotions effectively in other people, and so are persuasive. The most effective people sense   others' reactions and fine-tune their own responses to move interaction in the best direction. According to Goleman, star performers with this competence draw on a wider range of persuasion strategies than others do, including impression management, dramatic arguments or actions, and appeals to reason.

Communication is also a key competence in star performers. Possessing masterful communication skills enables a leader to grab the attention of his followers when he speaks. Steve Jobs had the ability to captivate people. He was good at storytelling. At the iPad launch, he created a scenario that helped viewers to imagine a Sunday-morning scene at home, using this new product while reading a paper. "Jobs then also started by opening the webpages of an American newspaper. By creating these stories in our head he communicates the advantages of his products most efficiently (David 2010).

Another key competence of leaders is conflict management, the ability to spot trouble as it is brewing and taking steps to calm those involved. Here the arts of listening and empathizing are crucial to the skills of handling difficult people and situations with diplomacy, encouraging debate and open discussion, and orchestrating win-win situations.

Research by the Hay Group, culled from its 17 000-person behavioural competency database in 2012, reveals that when it comes to empathy, influence and the ability to manage conflicts in the executive level, women show more skill than men. Specifically, women are more likely to show empathy as strength, demonstrate strong ability in conflict management, show skills in influence, and have a sense of self-awareness. I could not agree more with this, and other pieces of research that allude to the fact that women generally posses more EQ than men, even men who are hailed as the greatest innovators and CEOs. Let's look at Steve Jobs, the late CEO of Apple. Don't get me wrong; this is not a Steve-bashing section. Unlike First National Bank, who used a character named Steve in their advertising campaign and created a negative perception around this character, I have nothing against people with the name Steve. I am just using Mr. Jobs to make a point in case.

Jobs lacked empathy. In his interview with Fortune senior editor, Betsy Morris, he said, "My job is to not be easy on people. My job is to make them better. My job is to pull things together from different parts of the company and clear the ways and get the resources for the key projects. And to take these great people we have and to push them and make them even better, coming up with more aggressive visions of how it could be." (Jobs 2008)

A woman would have conveyed the same message, but differently. She would have chosen her words very carefully, to avoid coming out as arrogant or rude. In fact, chances are, a woman would have the said all the words in that paragraph, except for the first sentence.

Jobs' low level of empathy was also noticeable in his behaviour and actions. He would park his Mercedes in a handicapped space, sometimes taking up two spaces. "The pattern became so noticeable

that employees put notes on his windshield that read, Park Different."
(Taylor 2009)

Jobs also lacked self-control and tact. Once in a meeting, he asked, "Can anyone tell me what Mobile-Me is supposed to do?" Having received a satisfactory answer, he continued, "So why the fuck doesn't it do that?" For the next half-hour Jobs berated the group. "You've tarnished Apple's reputation," he told them. "You should hate each other for having let each other down." (Nocera 2011)

Jobs was also low on trustworthiness, which was defined earlier. Trustworthiness is all about letting others know your values and principles, intentions and feelings, and acting in ways that are consistent with them but Jobs made statements and then reneged on them. When he returned to Apple he said he did not want to be CEO, but he quickly took charge.

We have also mentioned earlier that trustworthy individuals are forthright about their own mistakes and confront others about their lapses. Jobs never admitted to his own mistakes. He was fault proof. He took credit for good work and blamed others for poor performance. In the documentary *Triumph of the Nerds*, he blames others for failures at Apple and redeemed himself. The famous quote by Ivan Illich – *"Leadership does not depend on being right"* – did not resonate with him.

One might ask, so what the heck? Steve Jobs was a great leader with the highest level of intelligence and expertise. He co-founded Apple and created products that were revolutionary, that nobody had even though of before. And he did a good job at that. Today, Apple's share remains on the top of the list. So, why the fuss about the fuzzy stuff?

Well, here is the answer. Whilst Jobs was successful in business, he was not an effective leader. Yes, he was intelligent, innovative and reasoned well. However, he lacked the humane qualities of effective leadership. He had no emotional intelligence. He was hungry for power and cared less about what other people though about him. He never focused on promoting harmony within the team, encouraging inclusion and resolving conflict.

Jobs' self-centred attitude created tension between him and his board, and resulted in him being ousted from the company he had co-founded. Although he was later re- instated, he became an "ED" (see the next chapter to find out about "ED"), before getting his job back. It was only towards the end of his second tenure at Apple that Jobs admitted that he lacked people skills and began to soften up a bit.

16.   SELF-AWARENESS

"Knowing others is intelligence, knowing yourself is true wisdom. Mastering others is strength, mastering yourself is true power." – Lao Tzu

Like authenticity, self-awareness (or personal mastery as others prefer to call it), is a key ingredient for successful women (and men) in leadership. In fact, the two are connected. Self-awareness is about knowing your abilities, shortcomings and opportunities for growth in order to be able to provide direction, guidance and inspiration to others. It is about understanding your actions and how you come across to others. Knowing your boundaries, values, and requirements from others allows you to improve relationships.

Self-awareness challenges us to think beyond the assumptions and beliefs that we know and that we use as our coping mechanisms when confronting life because, as Lao Tsu observed, much of our power is wasted in maintaining assumptions and beliefs, defending them and foisting them on other people. This stops us from seeing things as they are. We forfeit our power to change by using our power to stay the same (Yudelowitz, Koch et al. 2002).

When we insist on hiding behind our safe coping mechanism, we let assumptions and beliefs stand in our way of seeing things from other's perspectives. We even conform to the status quo. We leave things unquestioned, in order to avoid conflict and being disliked.
We leave matters unresolved   and relationships strained, creating uncomfortable feelings and fear in ourselves. We choose not to name the

issue. When we have fear, are unable to name the issue and resolve the conflict it may be causing, we become poor leaders. Being self-aware allows us to find the courage to name the issue and resolve conflict.

Self-awareness helps us build relationships. The more self-aware you are, the better you interact with others and the more you are able to lead effectively. In the military, a leader can get away with the "this is me, take me as I am" attitude. But in business, this is a seriously career-limiting move. You need to care about how others perceive you. You need to seek out feedback from others and be open to it, whether it is positive or negative. Today, most corporations perform 360-degree performance reviews, whereby not only your boss assesses you, but also the people you work with.

Companies, specifically boards, tend to hire external consultants to assess the suitability of a candidate for key leadership positions. Consider this encounter by Warren Bennis, founding chairman of the Leadership Institute: "I was asked to evaluate the number two executive in a large global corporation for the firm's top post. Let's call this executive Ed. He seemed ideal: energetic, ambitious, and super smart. It took me about six months to come to the conclusion that though Ed looked perfect, he lacked a crucial ingredient of leadership – integrity. Nobody trusted him, and I couldn't help him. But the board ignored my advice, and when the incumbent chief executive officer had a heart attack, in a collective panic the board elevated Ed. He was summarily discharged only twelve months later." (Bennis, Cherniss et al. 2003)

It is clear that Ed was intelligent and well-suited for the CEO post. But "nobody trusted him". Obviously, for Bennis to conclude that Ed was not trustworthy, he must have spoken to his colleagues and other people that he had done business with. The majority, if not all, of these people must have rated him very low on trustworthiness and integrity. Because he never received feedback about how people felt about him, he had no opportunity to rectify his shortcoming. He assumed the CEO position, only to be frog-marched out a year later. So, once again, trust emerges as a crucial element of self- awareness.

Self-awareness allows us to know our limitations and weaknesses. If we are aware of and admit to the things that we are not good at, we are able to better harness the power, skill and knowledge that other members of our teams have. We are able to let go of our pride and ego and ask for help, for the greater good of the organization. Often, we think that the answers lie outside, with expensive consultants. This is very common in South Africa, where corporations, particularly SEOs (State Owned Enterprises), spend billions of Rands on consultants (usually those from the US or the UK), as they believe that the answer lies somewhere else.

But the truth is, it always lies within. The diversity of expertise in a team means that someone might know something that we do not, and being able to tap into others' expertise is a great skill in leadership. As Jung once said, "We need others to be truly ourselves". When we help each other, when we truly team up, magic happens.

Self-awareness also allows us to not be victims of expectations. Often, we get trapped into being what we are not, in order to be accepted in society. Consider, for example, the case of Enron, whose CEO succumbed to dishonesty and unethical behaviour because he wanted to please analysts, investors, authors and consultants. The company was receiving good reviews and there was a lot of media hype from all corners. Meanwhile, the company was not doing so well and was actually facing bankruptcy. In order to meet the expectations of the outside world, the company started cooking the books.

When the company could no longer sustain the deceit, it was obliged to restate their earnings, a move the caused the company to collapse. Had the CEO and his leadership team been self-aware, they would have acknowledged that the company was failing and have admitted it, instead of resorting to fraudulent and unethical behaviour. Enron would not have been the first company in history to go bankrupt, and most importantly it would have not gone down in the business history books as the biggest corporate scandal of our time. It would have gone down with dignity, like many other companies before it.

Another challenge of living according to other's expectation is that we allow ourselves to be anaesthetised to our dreams and lose sight of our deeply felt Ideal Self. For example, your motivation of wanting to be in the C-Suite might be money and the glamour of the C-Titles. You may be measuring success in terms of money and position. However, deep inside, this may not really be what you want. You may secretly be wishing to be a nun or nurse. But, because those jobs do not come with wealth and prestige, you may be suppressing your real passion.

In today's business, where the media always profile successful women, stressing how they are the first woman CEO, President, Commercial Pilot, Industrial Engineer, Computer Scientist, and so on, we may be tempted to want to follow a career that no woman has branched into as yet. Our motivation for this decision might be that we also want to be the first women in that industry so that we can enjoy the attention that comes with being first. We would pursue this ambition, even when we have no passion or interest in that particular career.

By acting and behaving in a manner that does not really define us, such as following careers that do not really define who we are, we lose our ideal self. However, if we are self- aware, we defy the norm and other's expectations, and put ourselves first. We follow our passion. When we are passionate, we become effective leaders.

Sometimes, a personal tragedy such as death or a life- threatening illness allows us to be more self-aware by giving us a chance to reflect. For example, author Bill George (George 2003) writes about his wife Penny, who after being diagnosed with breast cancer, gave up her psychology practice to devote herself to integrative medicine. She became a tireless advocate for changing how medicine is taught and practised and took on leadership roles she never imagined (George

2003). She took time to re-evaluate what was important in her life.

Women should get a source of credible feedback. This could be a trusted colleague or your boss. Although the truth often hurts, it's the key to self-improvement. It is important to have people in your life who will keep you in perspective and give you honest feedback, so learn how to ask for advice and take feedback on board. Of her relationship with her boss, Mark Zuckenberg, Sheryl Sandberg said: "We sit next to each other, we Facebook message each other a lot. We give each other feedback every Friday."

Feedback is useful in assessing your behaviour and actions, then discarding the behaviour and actions that are detrimental to success and keeping those that contribute positively to it. One key lesson in using feedback to assess what improve your performance is to "take criticism seriously, but not personally." (Hillary Clinton)

Women should also realise that, as much as they have strengths, they have weaknesses too. Know your strong and weak points, and ask for help with the latter. You are not an all-rounder and you do not have superpowers. Remember that: *"No man will make a great leader who wants to do it all himself, or to get all the credit." Andrew Carnegie*

Another strategy for increasing self-awareness is meditation. Many different types of meditation have been taught that can be useful for helping people become more aware of how their emotions affect their behaviour. One of the more effective ones is mindfulness meditation, which is designed specifically to help people become more aware of their inner experience (Kabat-Zinn, 1990). (Bennis, Cherniss et al. 2003)

Once a leader has demonstrated authenticity, self- awareness and emotional awareness, they are in a position to start setting goals and visions and get their followers to buy into that vision, because "people buy into the leader before they buy into the vision" (John C. Maxwell). The next step would be to move towards focusing on visionary leadership, which is what the next chapter is about.

17. VISIONARY LEADERSHIP

"Good business leaders create a vision, articulate the vision, passionately own the vision, and relentlessly drive it to completion." –
Jack Welch

Many organizations' websites have a vision and mission. More often than not, the two are used interchangeably and yet they are different. Peter Senge, a guru of organizational development offers this distinction: a mission is a purpose and reason for being, whereas a vision is a picture or image of the future we seek to create. Creating a vision is one of the major tasks of leaders, hence Theodore M. Hesburgh has said: "The very essence of leadership is that you have to have vision. You can't blow an uncertain trumpet."

Visionary leadership is about creating the future. It is about the ability to think beyond the conventional, come up with unorthodox solutions, and serve colleagues, clients, and others in one's life with truly creative results. Creating the future develops uncommon yet highly practical ways to identify the most promising opportunities for personal and professional breakthroughs (Bennis, Cherniss et al. 2003). It encompasses the abilities to frame the current practices as inadequate, to generate ideas for new strategies, and to communicate possibilities in inspiring ways to others.

Visionary leaders draw on a range of personal skills to inspire others to work together toward common goals. They are able to articulate and arouse enthusiasm for a shared vision and mission. Excellent communication skills and trust are some of these personal attributes. Successful leaders use language artfully to describe their vision; people feel that, despite not always being able to see the possibilities it suggests, they are still able to suspend their anxiety and disbelief. They follow their leader into uncharted territory because they trust him or her, and therefore the vision itself (Bennis, Cherniss et al. 2003).

Visionary leaders articulate where a group is going, but not how it will get there. The leader focuses on setting people free to innovate, experiment and take calculated risks. He or she only steps forward as needed, to guide the performance of others while holding them accountable. A great example of a female visionary leader is Dolly Mokgatle, during her tenure at Spoornet. When she took over the entity, she adopted a "back-to-basics" strategy, as Spoornet had lost sight of the fundamentals of running a business and had no direction.

"I've always known that you derive greater benefits as a leader by harnessing good teams around you. If you can give those teams direction and empower them to do what they are there for, they'll fly,"
she said.

As has been pointed out in the previous chapters, women possess more leadership attributes and traits than men, including EQ. However, on the dimension of visionary leadership, men are perceived to lead the pack. They are perceived to have a greater ability to imagine different and better future conditions and ways to achieve them. The question is: Is this just a gender stereotypical perception, or is it a fact?

In their article titled *Women and the Vision thing*, Ibarra and Obudaru

(2009) found the answer. They concur that, as a group, women outshone men in most of the leadership dimensions measured. There was one exception, however, and it was a big one: Women scored lower on "envisioning"

– the ability to recognize new opportunities and trends in the environment and develop a new strategic direction for an enterprise.

In order to progress to middle and senior management, women focus on the technical elements of their jobs and on accomplishing quantifiable objectives. But they need to realize that, as they step into bigger leadership roles, the rules of the game change and a different set of skills comes to the fore. One of those new skills is the ability to sell their vision of the future to numerous stakeholders. Presenting an inspiring story about the future is very different from generating a brilliant strategic analysis or crafting a logical implementation plan.

"Management is efficiency in climbing the ladder of success; leadership determines whether the ladder is leaning against the right wall."
Stephen Covey

Ibarra and Obudaru (2009) tell the story of Anne Dumas, who focused technical expertise to double revenues and operating margins, in just five years as CEO. Ann was reluc- tant to adopt her holding company's male CEO's preference for visionary behaviour over technical substance. She said: "I always wonder what people mean when they say, 'He's not much of a manager but is a good leader.' Leader of what? You have to do things to be a leader." She went on to imply that so-called visionary behaviour might even be harmful. "We are in danger today of being mesmerized by people who play with our reptilian brain. For me, it is manipulation. I can do the storytelling too, but I refuse to play on people's emotions. If the string pulling is too obvious, I can't make myself do it." The sentiments of Dumas were shared by one of my respondents, a Marketing Director of a large media company, who said: "I decided long ago, before I became an executive, that I was going to compete on my skills and my abilities. I challenge myself and my worst critic is me."

Women need to realize that managing for continuous improvement to the status quo is different from being a force for change that compels a group to innovate and depart from routine. And if leadership is essentially about realizing change, then crafting and articulating a vision of a better future is a leadership prerequisite. No vision, no leadership. Women need to learn to be visionaries.

But women have come out to defend themselves against the perception that they lack vision. In the Ibarra and Obudaru (2009) study, women put forward three reasons why they may be wrongfully perceived as lacking visionary skills.

Firstly, the women said they have as much vision as men do, but they portray it in a different manner, which is less directive. One woman said: "Many women tend to be quite collaborative in forming their vision. They take into account the input of many and then describe the result as the group's vision rather than their own." Another said, "I don't see myself as particularly visionary in the creative sense. I see myself as pulling and putting together abstract pieces of information or observations that lead to possible strategies and future opportunities."

Due to their collaborative nature, women prefer to involve others in creating their vision. They also rely on diverse and external inputs and alliances. A case in point is BP CEO for Alternative Energy, Vivienne Cox, who spent much of her time talking to key people outside her business group and the company in order to develop a strategic perspective on opportunities and sell the idea of low-carbon power to her CEO and peers. A wide network, including thought leaders in a range of sectors, informed her ideas. She brought in outsiders who could transcend a parochial view to fill key roles and invited potential adversaries into the process early on to make sure those who had a different view of the world also informed her team.

This action, which was largely driven by women's collaborative leadership style, led Ibarra and Obudaru (2009) to the following interesting hypothesis: By involving their male peers in the process of creating a vision, female leaders may get less credit for the result.

Secondly, the women in the study said that they prefer to base their vision for the future on facts and not on improvable assertions. Due to the fact that women are presumed to be less competent than men, they prefer to extrapolate facts and figures to make a point, instead of going out on a limb. They prefer to rely less on their imagination and creativity and stick to safe choices.

To drive this point Ibarra and Obudaru (2009) refer to two Democratic candidates for the 2008 U. S. presidential race. Barack Obama was viewed as a visionary, a charismatic communicator offering a more hopeful if undetailed future. Hillary Clinton was viewed as a competent executor with an impressive if uninspiring grasp of policy detail. Clinton as much as admitted that she does not inspire through rhetoric and emotion and said: "A President, no matter how rhetorically inspiring, still has to show strength and effectiveness in the day-to-day handling of the job, because people are counting on that. So, yes, words are critically important, but they're not enough. You have to act. In my own experience, sometimes it's putting one foot in front of the other, day after day."

Lastly, the women in the study, like Dumas, did not put any value on being visionary. Ibarra and Obudaru (2009) found that women took pride in their concrete, no-nonsense attitude and practical orientation toward everyday work problems. The authors say they were reminded of a comment made by Margaret Thatcher: "If you want anything said, ask a man; if you want anything done, ask a woman." Like Anne Dumas, the women valued substance over form as a means of gaining credibility with key stakeholders. A pharmaceutical executive elaborated further: "I see women as more practical. Although the women in my organization are very strategic, they are also often the ones who ground the organization in what is possible, what can or cannot be done from the human dimension."

Women need to embrace visionary leadership. Yes technical skills and strategic know-how are crucial, but: "Leadership is a potent combination of strategy and character. But if you must be without one, be without the strategy." (Norman Schwarzkopf)

18. TRANSFORMATIONAL AND CHARISMATIC LEADERSHIP

We have already stressed that the whole point of leadership is to initiate change and that visionary thinking is crucial for initiating change. In order to carry out their role of transforming companies, leaders need charisma, oodles and oodles of charisma. As Jack and Suzy Welch said, charisma makes the leader's job much easier. Helping people to see the need for change and to be able to engage in activities that facilitate change is done faster with charisma than with fact, reasoning and logic. No amount of Excel spread sheets and PowerPoint slides can beat charisma in influencing people.

But what is charisma? It is a Greek work meaning "divinely inspired gift". Charismatic leaders have an exceptional gift for inspiration and communication. The term refers to a special quality of leaders whose purpose, powers and extraordinary determination differentiates them from others. In simple terms, charisma means charming, with a bubbly personality. It is a compelling attribute that creates a strong desire in followers to want to be led by that person because, when they speak, charismatic leaders leave their followers in awe, devotion and emotional dependence. Think of the pastors in charismatic churches, and you will have an idea of what I am on about.

Charismatic leaders are characterised by the ability to create vision and get others to buy into it, masterful communication skills, the ability to inspire trust and make group members feel capable, the ability to connect with people, willingness to take risk and a self-promoting personality. They also have energy and are action-oriented. Above all, they are dramatic and unique in significant, positive ways. Being dramatic does not mean being a drama queen. It is about having presence. It is about people feeling you and taking note when you enter the room. A good dress sense can help in creating a personal brand, thus creating uniqueness.

So, how do charismatic leaders manage to attract, motivate and lead others? How do they get others to willingly want to follow them and do as the leader asks them? A lot of this has got to do with how charismatic leaders communicate. Typically, they have a colourful, imaginative and expressive manner of putting their message across. They use metaphors and analogy to inspire their audience. As they know that various groups of constituents have varying degrees of verbal sophistication, they gear language to different audiences. How they speak to business analyst is different from how they speak to factory workers.

Storytelling is another effective communication tool that charismatic leaders use. This refers to a unique manner of inspiring audiences by telling fascinating stories. A well- crafted story always captures people's attention. It is no wonder that companies are now hiring outside consultants to coach their executives on storytelling

Charisma is a component of transformational leadership

– another leadership attribute that is crucial for today's leaders. Transformational leaders are those who bring about major, positive change in an organization. According to DuBrin (2013), transformational leadership focuses on what the leader accomplishes, yet still pays attention to the leader's personal characteristics and his or her relationship with group members. In other words, the essence of transformational leadership is the developing and transforming of people.

Transformational leaders set expectations and achieve greater results by challenging their followers to be more innovative. The transformational leader helps bring about major, positive changes by moving group members beyond their self-interest and towards the good of the group, organization or society. The essence of transformational leadership is developing and transforming. Leaders are only effective in developing and transforming people, if they have "charisma".

Vinkenburg, van Engen et al. (2011) argue that women score higher in transformational leadership than men. Based on this, one would expect that more women would be occupying top positions in the C-suite. However, this is not the case because decision-makers regard inspirational motivation, the transformational leadership factor at which men score highest, as being the most valuable in C-suite selection decisions. By contrast, women score higher on the individualised consideration factor, which is only perceived as more important for promotion into senior management positions.

Young women should work on building their natural charisma. Research shows that women have natural charisma – the charm that makes people want to stop, take note of you and listen to what you have to say, with great enthusiasm. But let us not fool ourselves, not every woman has these attributes.

19. ETHICAL LEADERSHIP

The complexity of today's complex business environment is not only a result of the tough external environment, such as globalization, high fuel prices and currency fluctuations. Ethics, sustainability and governance present as much a challenge for today's leader. Sustainable development, a development that meets the needs of the present without compromising the ability of future generations to meet their own needs, has become a buzzword in business today. Corporate governance refers to systems of principles and practices and internal structures, by which the firm ensures accountability and transparency to its stakeholders in a manner that helps to ensure the ongoing, sustainable economic performance of the firm.

The latest corporate scandals, such as the Enron one that we discussed earlier on, that have been driven by a lack of ethics and morals, indicate that there is a leadership crisis facing today's leaders.

Often, leaders who compromise good governance principles and succumb to unethical behaviour are believers in the views of liberal economists, who argue that the role of business decision makers is to focus on making profits and creating value for shareholders. As Nobel Laureate Milton Friedman put it in 1970, "The social responsibility of business is to increase its profit" (Friedman 2007). Friedman's position has been largely criticised for failing to take into consideration the critical need for organizations to conduct business in a sustainable manner.

As a result, there has been a shift towards a new business model, which emphasises that true, sustainable corporate citizenship is built on the triple bottom line – People, Planet, Profit – or the triple P. The PPP model is based on the premise that companies make profit not in isolation but within communities and the environment, and therefore businesses should share their wealth with communities and the environment, in order to sustain themselves. Organizations are now aware that "the economic self-interest as the primary or even the only motivation for business is out of place." (Sen 1997)

So, what kind of a leader is needed to uphold good governance and drive sustainability? Reul Khoza, one of South Africa's prominent corporate leaders and author of *Let Africa Lead*, suggests Attuned Leadership. The attuned leader is an insightful person who stresses the importance of human relationships, empathising and identifying with their followers, winning their trust and producing results in line with the needs of the followers. Therefore, attuned leadership provides a compass for the direction of ethical leadership. Life, work and moral values are indivisible – particularly for those in positions of leadership.

At the centre of attuned leadership is the concept of Ubuntu or African humanism. Ubuntu is a Zulu word that is based on the proverb "*umuntu ngumuntu ngabantu*", which loosely translated means "*I am what I am because of who we all are*". African humanism or Ubuntu evokes both reason and empathy as the basis for ethical leadership. In other words, it is a valued-based type of leadership. According to Khoza, the reciprocal relationship between the individual and the social collective stimulates caring and progressive thought and action.

Khoza maintains that a leader who is not attuned to his or her followers soon becomes a leader in limbo and invariably then fails. Connectedness, compassion, empathy, integrity, humility, reasonableness and a determination to be effective are the keys to attuned leadership. An attuned leader can step boldly into an uncertain future with the certainty that followers will lend their support.

When a leader is honest and humble enough to admit to his mistakes, he is likely to get support from his followers and, with this support, he is able to learn from his mistakes and move forward to achieve greater results. The temptation to get involved in unethical behaviour to cover up his mistakes is greatly reduced. In Khoza's own words:

"Leaders cannot ignore growing global crisis, but neither can they act unless they have the support from behind and below. Attuned leadership, in our current circumstances, requires honesty from the leadership and pressure from the followership."

young women need to build strong relationships and surround themselves with people who have the skills that they do not have and who will be willing to keep them on track when the pressure to behave unethically builds up.

20. CROSS – CULTURAL LEADERSHIP

With the advent of globalisation and international management, the world of business has become more complex and a new set of challenges has emerged. As global managers move from their home countries into new territories as expatriates and international assignees or simply as short-term visitors pitching ideas for international business opportunities, they are faced with a huge cultural gap. This cultural gap is underpinned by cultural stereotypes, global variations in business practices and communication. It is important to note that this chapter is about national culture (country-level) and not corporate culture (organizational- level).

Hofstede (1980) defines culture as the collective programming of the mind, which distinguishes the members of one human group to another and Spencer-Oatey (2000) defines it as a fuzzy set of attitudes, beliefs, behavioural norms and basic assumptions and values that are shared by a group of people and that influence each member's behaviour and his/her interpretations of the "meaning of other people's behaviour". Simply put, culture is a set of shared values, principles and beliefs that guide the thinking and behaviour of a group of individuals. It is particular to one group and not others.

Within and among cultures, diversity does exist. However, in each single culture certain behaviours are favoured and others are repressed. So, in the end, the group behaves in uniform and predictable ways. But why is national culture important in international business?

When I did an International Business module at the university of Warwick in the UK, as part of my MBA studies, students were involved in an interesting simulation that involves a group of Americans from a large multinational pharmaceutical company and the Amberana, a small tribe in a tiny rural village outside the US. The Americans had discovered that the Amberana had a mystery plant that could be used to cure a certain life-threatening illness. Getting this plant would result in billions of revenue for them. But they had to visit the Amberana and negotiate with them to get the plant. Negotiations deadlocked due to cultural nuances. For example, during the negotiations, the American sat on chairs and not on the floor like their hosts. The Amberana felt offended by this and saw this is the highest form of disrespect.

It is no secret that in order to be able to negotiate successfully and attain great business performance, multinational organizations must learn to adapt their practices to those of the countries in which they wish to do business. Understanding culture helps managers to understand and make sense of the international environment that they wish to or already operate in. It is crucial to consider the consequences of different cultural preferences on business processes, communication and practices.

The best place to start in ascertaining the culture of a foreign country is to determine whether it is High Context (HC) or Low Context (LC) culture. Hall (1976) and Kim et al (1998) provide the following distinctions between the two.

Firstly, in a HC culture, people are deeply involved with each other through lots of shared experiences, and relationships are valued and last for a long time. Information is widely shared through simple messages with deep meaning. Great distinction is made between insiders and outsiders and relationships are based on connections. There is a high level of commitment and people's word to complete tasks is often followed through. People generally avoid confrontation to maintain peace and intimate bonds. Minor disagreements are ignored and inner feelings are repressed. Communication is mostly through non-verbal signals.

By contrast, in an LC culture, people are highly individualised. It is everybody for him or herself. Relationships are shorter and alienated. Communication is explicit. The listener knows very little and gets told everything in detail. There is a thin line between insiders and outsiders. Foreigners are not made to feel like outsiders and they adjust quickly into new cultures. People do not usually feel bound to complete actions and so there is a need for an enforceable contract that binds them. Confrontation and criticism are direct and face-saving is not tolerated. Communication is explicit and what is important is what is said and not how it is said.

Consider the following example from the module that I referred to earlier. A Westerner asked a Chinese HR Director, "Do you think Mr Sim will be able to come to the course next week as I would like to make a hotel reservation for him and the hotel is quite full?" The Chinese HR Director answered, "It is possible he may have to attend a meeting in Shanghai". Two days later, just before the course began, the Westerner followed up with an email and asked, "I am following up my earlier conversation and am wondering if Mr Sim will be attending the course". The Chinese replied, "As I told you previously, he will NOT attend". This was a significant misunderstanding between people from two different cultures, resulting in the HR director ignoring the Westerner at work for several days.

Language is equally critical when working in a multi- cultural environment. When I was a brand manager for one of the brands I worked with, we used a Portuguese word that means freedom for our campaign in Angola and Mozambique, both of which are Portuguese-speaking countries. The word was well receive in Angola, but was perceived to be in bad taste in Mozambique, as the country had just come out of a civil war and did not want to be reminded of that painful period, which was characterised by the word that we used.

Even a simple thing like reasoning differs from culture to culture. According to Erin Meyer, a professor at INSEAD and author of *The Culture Map: Breaking Through The Invisible Boundaries of Global Business,* there are two basic styles of reasoning: Principles-first reasoning, where you establish the "why" before you move to the "what"; and Applications-first reasoning, where you start with the "what" before the "why". For example, when a manager is tasked with assessing a business challenge and offer recommendations, Italians will be interested in finding out why (before the recommendations are laid out to them). They want the background/analysis to the problem, the basis for the recommendations and the methodology used. Americans, on the other hand, might want you save them the long explanations, get to the point and tell them what will happen if the recommendations are effected. Otherwise, they will disengage.

In Africa, we seem to place a great deal of value on personal relationships, caring for each other and working together towards the achievement of the greater good. The concept of Ubuntu, that we referred to earlier, is what defines African Leadership.

The secret to cross-cultural management is to find out as much as you can about the national culture of the country that you do business in, embrace it, respect it and adapt to it. By so doing, you are demonstrating to your host country that you value them.

21. CONCLUSION

In their 2008 study, in which more than 1 000 executives from nine countries (all alumni of executive education programs) were asked for their impressions of men and women in general as leaders, Catalyst researchers Jeanine Prime and Nancy Carter, and IMD professors Karsten Jonsen and Martha Maznevski, found that both men and women tended to believe that the two genders have distinct leadership strengths, with women out-scoring men on some behaviour, and men out-scoring women on others. In fact, women out-scored men on most elements tested.

The previous chapters also alluded to the fact that leadership experts also agree that women are naturally gifted with key attributes of transformational leadership, charismatic leadership, emotional intelligence and authentic leadership. But, if women are naturally more suited to becoming better leaders than men, why are there still so few of them in C-Suite and boardrooms?

Here is the reason. Brace yourself. In the same study by Jonsen and Mazvevski, when people were asked to rate the behaviour's relative importance to overall leadership effectiveness, the "male" behaviours had the edge. Across countries, "inspiring others" – a component of our envisioning dimension – landed at the top of the rankings as most important to overall leadership effectiveness. And what of the areas of leadership where men agreed that women were stronger? Let's take women's standout advantage: their much greater skill at "supporting others". That one ranked at the bottom of the list. As a component of overall leadership effectiveness, it was clearly not critical but merely nice to have.

This is not surprising. As we have shown earlier, women are not perceived to be great visionaries and they rely on technical expertise and logic to lead. The sad thing is that women do not put great value on vision and tend to undermine its impact on leading people. Vision, as researchers and experts on leadership agree, is the essence of leadership. It is the key differentiator between a leader and an exceptional leader. You may have technical and cognitive skills, empathy, charisma, emotional intelligence and self-awareness and the highest level of ethics, but these are not sufficient. If you cannot paint a perfect picture for your followers to see where you would like to take them, you will not be a success as a leader. You may just as well become a follower too.

The case of Steve Jobs is a case in point. Although he was rude, not empathetic and never cared much about other people, he was a visionary. He mastered the art of leading by inspiration. His excellent communication skills and charisma enabled him to share his vision in an inspiring manner, getting him followers that were ready, willing and able to follow the path he had created for success.

Therefore, the challenge facing women is to stop undermining the impact of vision. Women need to realise that, while technical expertise got them into senior management, it will not get them into top management. Vision, on the hand will, and the lack of it is the only thing that is holding women back. Women need to start focusing their time and energy on the vision thing. Fortunately, being visionary, like all the other crucial elements of being an efficient member of the C-Suite, is a competency that can be developed.

I hope this book has given you some hints and tips to position yourself for the C-Suite position that you so want. Now is the time for you to digest it, reflect on it and start acting. Get yourself into that line job, network with the boys, get a mentor, lean in, review your leadership style, prioritise your choices about when to have children and when to build your career and, most of all, work on being a visionary. Nature has already blessed you with traits of leadership. So, appreciate them, build on them and create your own opportunities. You can do it! Go on, and become the best C-Suite leader that you can.

The recent news that Hillary Clinton is campaigning for US presidency in the next elections has been met with great joy by most women. It is refreshing to see an election campaign that is not cluttered by men in suits and ties, telling voters to vote for them. In contrast to her last campaign, Clinton is putting gender at the forefront of her message to voters. She has come to realise that positioning herself as a woman who is capable of running the White House, might just get her those votes. You too, should go out there, embrace your womanhood and position yourself as a woman who is capable of running an organization.

As a concluding thought, I leave you with this quote:

"I always did something I was a little not ready to do. I think that's how you grow. When there's that moment of 'Wow, I'm not really sure I can do this,' and you push through those moments, that's when you have a breakthrough." Marissa Mayer, CEO of Yahoo!

JUST PUT YOUR BEST FOOT FORWARD!

REFERENCES

Antal, A. B. and D. N. Izraeli (1993). "A global comparison of women in management: Women managers in their homelands and as expatriates."

Barreto, M. E., et al. (2009). The glass ceiling in the 21st century: Understanding barriers to gender equality, American Psychological Association.

Barsh, J. and L. Yee (2012). "Unlocking the full potential of women at work." Wall Street Journal.

Bennis, W., et al. (2003). The emotionally intelligent workplace: How to select for, measure, and improve emotional intelligence in individuals, groups, and organizations, John Wiley & Sons.

Bilhuber Galli, E. and G. Müller-Stewens (2012). "How to build social capital with leadership development: Lessons from an explorative case study of a multibusiness firm." The Leadership Quarterly 23(1): 176-201.

Bourdieu, P. (1990). The logic of practice, Stanford University Press.

Carli, L. L. (2006). "Gender issues in workplace groups: Effects of gender and communication style on social influence." Gender and communication at work: 69-83.

Cohen, W. A. (2000). The new art of the leader: Leading with integrity and honor, Prentice Hall Press.

Cook, J., et al. (1994). "Partners in Learning: Redefining Mentorship for a learning Organization." South African Journal of Business Management **25**(3).

David, K. (2010). Leadership behaviours and Attitudes of Steve Jobs. Day, D. V. and J. Antonakis (2012). The nature of leadership, Sage.

Day, D. V. and M. M. Harrison (2007). "A multilevel, identity-based approach to leadership development." Human Resource Management Review **17**(4): 360-373.

De Pater, I. E., et al. (2010). "Gender differences in job challenge: a matter of task allocation." Gender, Work & Organization **17**(4): 433-453.

Dezsö, C. L. and D. G. Ross (2012). "Does female representation in top management improve firm performance? A panel data investigation." Strategic Management Journal **33**(9): 1072-1089.

DuBrin, A. J. (2010). Principles of leadership, South-Western Canada. DuBrin, A. J. (2013). Principles of leadership, South-Western Cengage

Learning.

Eagly, A. H. and L. L. Carli (2007). Through the labyrinth: The truth about how women become leaders, Harvard Business

Press.

Eagly, A. H. and L. L. Carli (2007). "Women and the labyrinth of leadership." Harvard business review **85**(9): 62.

Eagly, A. H. and M. C. Johannesen-Schmidt (2001). "The leadership styles of women and men." Journal of Social Issues **57**(4): 781-797.

Eagly, A. H. and S. J. Karau (2002). "Role congruity theory of prejudice toward female leaders." Psychological review **109**(3): 573.

Evans, C. D. and A. B. Diekman (2009). "On motivated role selection: Gender beliefs, distant goals, and career interest." Psychology of Women Quarterly **33**(2): 235-249.

Fitzsimmons, T. W., et al. (2014). "Gender disparity in the C-suite: Do male and female CEOs differ in how they reached the top?" The Leadership Quarterly **25**(2): 245-266.

Friedman, M. (2007). The social responsibility of business is to increase its profits, Springer.

Furst, S. A. and M. Reeves (2008). "Queens of the hill: Creative destruction and the emergence of executive leadership of women." The Leadership Quarterly **19**(3): 372-384.

George, B. (2003). Authentic Leadership: Rediscovering the Secrets to Creating lasting Value, Jossey-Bass.

Giscombe, K. (2007). "Women in corporate leadership: status and prospects." Women and leadership. The state of play and strategies for change.

Guay, F., et al. (2003). "Academic self-concept and academic achievement: Developmental perspectives on their causal ordering." Journal of educational psychology **95**(1): 124.

Hewitt, S. A. and M. Marshall (2013). Women Want Five Things. C. f. T. Innovation, London School of Business.

Holgersson, C. (2001). "The social construction of top executives." Howard, C. (2011). "The World's 100 Most Powerful Women: This Year

It's All About Reach." Forbes. com.

Humphrey, J. (2014). "The Communication Style You Need to Break into The Old Boys' Club." Fast Company.

Hymowitz, C. (2004). "Through the glass ceiling." Wall Street Journal

116: R1.

Ibarra, H. (2012). "To close the Gender Gap, Focus on Assignments." Havard Business Review.

Ibarra, H. and O. Obudaru (2009). "Women and the Vision Thing." Havard Business Review.

Jobs, S. (2008). Jobsqna. CNN. B. Morris.

Kark, R., et al. (2012). "Does valuing androgyny and femininity lead to a female advantage? The relationship between gender-role, transformational leadership and identification." The Leadership Quarterly **23**(3): 620-640.

Klaus, P. (2009). A sisterhood of Workplace Infighting. New York

Times.

New York.

Kray, L. and M. Hasselhuhn (2012). "Male pragmatism in negotiators' ethical reasoning." Journal of Experimental Psychology(48).

Lyness, K. S. and D. E. Thompson (2000). "Climbing the corporate ladder: do female and male executives follow the same route?" Journal of Applied Psychology **85**(1): 86.

McKinsey (2011). "Changing Companies' minds about Women." MCKinsey Quarterly.

McKinsey (2013). Women Matter: Gender Diversity in Top Management

– Moving Corporate Culture, Moving Boundaries.

Mckinsey (2014). Why gender diversity at the top remains a challenge.

Miles, J. (2015). "The five things I want to tell employers about women returning to work." Guardian. com.

Morgan, W. M., et al. (1988). Lessons of experience: How successful executives develop on the job, Simon and Schuster.

Nocera, J. (2011). "Steve Jobs broke every leadership rule. Don't try that yourself.". from http://www. forbes. com/sites/ frderickallen/2011/08/27/steve-jobs-broke-every-leadership-rule- don't-try-that-yourself.

Northouse, P. (2012). Leadership: Theory and Practice.
Northouse, P. (2013). Leadership: Theory and Practice,

Sage Publications.

Oakley, J. G. (2000). "Gender-based barriers to senior management positions: Understanding the scarcity of female CEOs." Journal of business ethics **27**(4): 321-334.

Ohlott, P. J., et al. (1994). "Gender differences in managers' developmental job experiences." Academy of Management Journal **37**(1): 46-67.

Pallier, G. (2003). "Gender differences in the self-assessment of accuracy on cognitive tasks." Sex Roles **48**(5-6): 265-276.

Phelan, J. E., et al. (2008). "Competent yet out in the cold: Shifting criteria for hiring reflect backlash toward agentic women." Psychology of Women Quarterly **32**(4): 406-413.

Reskin, B. F. and D. B. McBrier (2000). "Why not ascription? Organizations' employment of male and female managers." American sociological review: 210-233.

Ruderman, M. N. and S. Ragolsky (2014). "Getting Real – How High Achieving Women can Lead Authentically." Centre for Creative Leadership.

Sandberg, S. (2013). "Lean In: Women, Work and the Will to Lead." Work, and the Will to Lead (Alfred A. Knopf).

Schein, V. E., et al. (1996). "Think manager—think male: A global phenomenon?" Journal of Organizational Behavior **17**(1): 33-41.

Sen, A. (1997). "Economics, business principles and moral sentiments." Business Ethics Quarterly **7**(3): 5-15.

Slaughter, A.-M. (2012). "Why Women Still Can't have it All." The Atlantic(July/Agust 2012).

Stadler, C. (2015). "How to Become a CEO." Forbes. com.

Stuckey, C. (2014). "6 Ways To Get Women in Leadership Positions and Keep them There." Fast Company.

Taylor, B. (2009). Decoding Steve Jobs. Trust the Art, not the Artist.

Tran, M. (2014). "Apple and Facebook to freeze eggs for female employees." The guardian.

Vinkenburg, C. J., et al. (2011). "An exploration of stereotypical beliefs about leadership styles: is transformational leadership a route to women's promotion?" The Leadership Quarterly **22**(1): 10-21.

WEF (2013). "Global Gender Gap Report." from http://www. weforum. org/issues/global-gender-gap.

Welch, J. (2012). "Women in the Economy." Wall Street Journal. Yudelowitz, J., et al. (2002). Smart things to know about leadership,

Capstone.